To Ray,
With Best Wishes,

THIS ISLAND LIFE

A Collection of Local Tales and Short Stories

From

The County Press 'Wight Memories'
and
The Beacon Magazine 'Island Story'

by

Brian Greening   *and*   *Alan Stroud*

Brian Greening   *Alan Stroud*

Now And Then Books 2019

Printed by Short Run Press

Introduction

Brian and Alan have been contributors to the 'Wight Memories' feature in the *County Press* for the past five years, Brian beginning in 2014 and Alan joining him in 2017 after he had spent five happy years at the *Beacon* magazine writing the 'Island Story' feature. In the past, they have ploughed their own furrows but they were always aware of each other's work and swapped notes and photographs on many occasions but largely went their own sweet ways. Until now.

Over the years, despite their different styles, a mutual admiration society grew up between them and the culmination of this affair is this collection of past articles by them both. Their articles, when they first appeared in the *County Press* or the *Beacon*, had a shelf life of just a week or two before ending up at the bottom of a parrot's cage. Indeed, if it had been seventy years earlier they would have been torn into squares and hung over a nail in the outside privy.

We felt either ending would have been a bit of a waste so we are giving them a second outing and a chance for immortality. Readers who are older than they care to admit might well remember Jack Hargreaves and his 'Out of Town' programmes on Southern Television. He had the gift of imparting knowledge by choosing interesting subjects and knowing his stuff. The end result was that when he'd finished, you'd learnt something – but you didn't feel like you'd spent two hours in a classroom. We hope our articles have the same effect now and again with our own wanderings and musings - if the feedback that we have received over the years is correct, we have. Bringing these articles together into one book seemed the right thing to do and we hope readers will agree.

Along the way we have had help from :

Sarah Griffin, Rachael Rosewell, Claire Willis, Simone Wilkinson, Colin Fairweather, Keir Foss, Alan Marriott, Keith Newbery, Tom Stroud, James Woolven and Richard Wright.

Brian : When Alan suggested to me that we compile this book we agreed that we would probably never have written any of the articles without the inspiration of the late Keith Newbery. He was a larger than life character with a great sense of humour. With Keith humour was never far away. He had a great love of sport, and was a man able to stand up in front of a large audience and tell stories. He had no trouble laughing at himself and often highlighted the mistakes he had made during the early years of his life spent in the newspaper industry, especially when he was a junior reporter. My favourite one was when as a raw junior he was sent to write a story on an unexploded bomb that had washed up on Southsea beach. His headline read, "Shell Found on Southsea Beach."

He was a wizard with words and went into raptures on the odd occasion that I sent him one that he had never encountered, such as when I passed him a story of the time a cargo of buffalo hides was washed up on a beach at the back of the Wight. Many of these were later sold to a Newport man who dealt in leather goods and who was later prosecuted for handling stolen goods. His occupation given in court was that of a "tawer." Keith was mystified but a look in his oldest dictionary told him that such a man was a "dresser of white leather."

Equally he would become irritated if people spelt his name incorrectly, as I did several times, variants including Newberry and Newbury. I remember telling him, when he berated me for the umpteenth time, to change his name to Smith.

He was a devoted family man, proud of his Island roots and unafraid to take on the 'establishment' if need be. I was once told that at the end of our lives most people can count on the fingers of one hand those whom they can call their true friends. I would name five whom I would choose as companions on a desert island, and without doubt I would have taken Keith with me as one of those five. So thank you Keith.

What follows, from my point of view, is all your fault!

Alan : Sadly, I didn't get to know Keith until about 2010. It began when I met him in the *County Press* foyer one day and passed a pleasant half hour chatting with him. That conversation led to Keith reviewing my next book in his column and from there we moved on to swapping emails about anything and everything.

At one point I told Keith I was nervous about the content of a forthcoming book of mine which was going to be critical of the *County Press* over some of its reporting of the festivals in the sixties. I was uneasy because the management, in the form of then Managing Director, Robin Freeman, had been so very helpful to me while I was researching the book. They had given me invaluable help in all manner of ways, including giving me out-of-hours access to their archives and I felt distinctly uncomfortable about putting the boot in after they had given me so much help. I sought Keith's opinion - his revealing reply was typical of the man :

"The County Press coverage of Bembridge Harbour and the pop festivals was scandalous and is indicative of what can happen if a local newspaper becomes embedded within the establishment. In 25 years as an editor, I never accepted any lunch, dinner or social invitations from any MPs or councillors. I was the only local newspaper editor in the country to turn down an invitation to meet the Queen at Windsor Castle when the Royals were mounting an affection offensive following the death of Diana. I am not making a bid for canonisation; merely pointing out how strongly I feel about where a local newspaper's priorities should lie. I have given the attitude of the CP in years past a reproving cuff around the ears a few times in my column and it has always gone in as written. Go ahead."

I did go ahead. In 2014 I was able to thank Keith for his kindness, and generous reviews of my books in the *County Press*, by preparing the artwork for his homage to Havenstreet, *God's Own Acre*, a book he co-wrote with Angela Snow.

I can only echo Brian's sentiments and say, "Thank you, Keith."

Finally, 'This Island Life,' was the title of Keith's column in the *County Press*. We're sure Keith would approve of the fact that we have shamelessly stolen the title from him. His love of all things Island was every bit as great as ours and it is just another small way of remembering a truly lovely man.

This was the last column ever to appear under Keith's byline :

August 8 2014

This Island life I loved

My grateful thanks for all your memories and anecdotes as I go to discover God's infinite acres

This column was written by Mark Newbery, son of Keith, with great inspiration from his dad as the two held hands during Keith's final hours. We hope it finds a special place in your hearts and offers some closure for the many readers who helped make Keith one of the most appreciated men on the Island. God bless you all.

Keith Newbery

It seems God was so happy with my recently released book and toil of love, *God's Own Acre*, that He unexpectedly decided to share His other infinite acres with me as well. It's quite a bit sooner than I would have liked but what an amazing place it is here! I can't tell you too much, there's a directive that personal discovery is the only path to enlightenment, it sounds so new-age I know, but this time I'm going to break with tradition and abide by the rules. The narrow lanes of Havenstreet's heavenly parallel are bustling with so many of the shiny-happy faces I've written of in columns past it's like a scene from one of my favourite films, Field of Dreams. I've not seen any of them since they took the long journey themselves, some recent, some long ago, so this reluctant transition has some privileges, even though it came too soon. I'm sorry I didn't get a chance to formally close this column with you all but life works in ways none of us can predict. It's safe to say I had years of anecdotes and observations left, not to mention material from all the brilliant submissions from my faithful readers, whom I hold dear and whose loyalty has always left this modest hack pleasantly bemused, but alas it wasn't to be. To those who wrote in opposition to my views, I thank you as well, because polarity is what makes life interesting and, if nothing else, you've allowed yourselves to be the brunt of a belly laugh or two over the years and you know what they say about laughter being the best tonic. No matter what your reason for reading or writing in, I thank you all for the stories and for the memories we shared together. After all, the essence of life is the accumulation of memories, big ones like getting married, becoming a parent, or, in my case most recently, a proud grandparent, and the smaller, everyday ones that become part of a rich tapestry of life, so take my word for it, keep accumulating them and stitch yourselves a beautiful quilt. To my friends, many of whom have been mentioned on this page over the years (Malc and the Winter brothers certainly had multiple appearances) I'm so sorry I had to go, I'm happy here but not happy that I journeyed far too soon and with such dizzying speed. Know that I am well and that other adventures await us in time but, please, for now, carry on enjoying all this life offers and you have my fervent permission to share stories and memories of me; I still want to be able to make you laugh, no matter what side of life I may walk. To my family, I love you all and I thank you for battling alongside me. I know it wasn't easy but in the end all that really matters is love and of that you allowed me to surf out on a tidal wave. It has been an absolute privilege to be your son, brother, husband, dad, and to my little Betsy, grampy; two years in the title wasn't enough but know that I loved you a lifetime's worth. My family, know that I treasured every moment of every stage of my life and that the love I have for you all is abundant beyond the sum of every letter and character I ever typed in 48 years of journalism and it will endure until we renew it again on God's infinite acres.

In the same issue, this letter from Brian appeared :

From Brian Greening, Newport:

Keith's passing leaves a huge gap in our lives

IN THE days before television, the radio was our sole means of entertainment and people would tune in and listen to their favourite programmes without a clue as to what the person who was talking to them looked like. All they wanted was to be entertained and kept informed and, hopefully, amused. To many Islanders, Keith Newbery was like one of those old radio entertainers. Each week for the past seven years he has come into the homes of Islanders, entertained them, made them laugh and occasionally infuriated them with a particularly outspoken comment. I doubt, however, if five per cent of those who read Keith's column every week had ever met him. They may have seen the tiny head and shoulders photo of him at the top of his column but they never knew that much about him. Those people were, sadly, the real losers. I got to know Keith very well through our interest in local history and sport and I am very glad I did. He was a larger-than-life character, an exceptional journalist and a fun guy to be with. I would spend many happy hours at Newclose Cricket Ground in his company and his friend, Malc Lawrence. In three hours we would put the government right on such things as gay marriages and illegal immigrants, criticise the cricketers when they only ran a single when it would have been easier to run two, moan about the weather, ridicule me for ten minutes when he saw I was wearing "Grumpy old Git" socks (a present from my grandchildren) and then turn on poor Malc for a bit of entertainment. In between, he would get through a large plate of salad. We were both born and bred on the Island, and proud of it, a fact we never ceased to tell people. Keith's love of Havenstreet persuaded him to become co-author of a book about the history of the village, he called God's own acre. When in company, we have been known to convince someone who has only been resident here for a couple of years, and who obviously does not share our love of all things rural, that new schemes were afoot. One was the cure for the Island's parking problems which was issuing driving licences only to those born on the Island. The reaction was always what we sought - indignation, then an

embarrassed look when the penny dropped that we were winding them up. Life in Keith's company was never dull and there was plenty of what I term "Isle of Wight humour" which can sometimes be interpreted as sarcasm but done in the best possible taste. If he couldn't do you a favour, he would never do you any harm. I attended evenings when he would give talks about his life in journalism and of his ill-fated performance of the television programme 'The Chase'. He loved his sport but cricket was his first love. It goes without saying how sad we all were to hear of Keith's death. I feel sure the County Press readers, even those who never met him, will join me in sending our condolences to Keith's wife and family. He has left an enormous gap in so many people's lives and it will take us all a long time to come to terms with the fact we shall not see him anymore. However, knowing him, when he arrives at the Pearly Gates, he will tell them he doesn't want to come in unless he can be captain of the cricket team. Such is the size and the persuasive nature of the man that I feel sure he will get his wish.

Sunshine and laughter - life was a beach and I shared this one with son Mark, behind.

by Brian Greening

The site near the barracks gates at Newport where Irish soldier James Artegan was hanged for robbery.

Prosperity - and trouble - were brought in equal measure by more than 7,000 troops that could be stationed in Newport when it was a garrison town. These troops spent their wages in the shops and in the public houses, and they provided customers for the many "ladies of the night." On the downside, however, this led to them stealing, getting drunk, fighting and brawling in the streets, and occasionally committing murder. Public houses were often the venue for such deeds and records show that the Castle Inn and the Shoulder of Mutton were two places where such offences were committed. A third was the Dolphin Inn in Sea Street, where in April 1800, two soldiers of the North Hants militia by the names of John Light and George Sainsbury, were having a quiet drink. A group of five Dutch soldiers strode in, and rival soldiers and alcohol are an inflammatory mix. The soldiers were Dirk Dollemans, Dirk Kochebakker, Jan Van Zyl, Jan Van Moor and Hendrick Koenfewere. Soon an argument took place and it was the latter who drew his sword and killed both the English soldiers and badly injured a barman. The Dutch soldiers were taken to the nearby Bridewell gaol but it was only Koenfewere who was charged, but he was quickly acquitted and was very soon sent back home.

Young lads outside the barracks at Parkhurst, now the site of
Albany prison, taken around 1897.

A few days later a donation that amounted to over £300 was made by the Dutch soldiers stationed at Parkhurst to the dependents of those killed, that I am told today would equate to around £25,000. This was made up of one day's pay from every Dutch soldier stationed at Parkhurst. The men were buried with full military honours and the Dutch brigade marched with the British troops in the funeral procession to the cemetery. It was here that a few months later the officers of the North Hants Militia had a headstone erected to their two dead colleagues. It read as follows :

> As over this tomb some sorrowing comrade stands,
> And mourns our lives, cut off by foreign hands,
> As fancy views this 'recking blade around,
> And live warm current rushing from the wounds,
> Let him exclaim with many grief opprest,
> Here unoffending murdered victims rest,
> Oh may our fate in warning accents show,
> What mischief from ungoverned passions flow.

However, the sometimes unevenly weighted scales of justice ensured that in 1814, an Irish soldier by the name of James Artegan felt the full force of the law after the Dutch soldier had escaped it. Artegan was a member of the York Chasseurs, a regiment with a fascinating pedigree. Formed in November 1813 by King George III, it was made up of what was described as "the better class of culprits and deserters," some being stationed on prison ships in the River Medina. This was not a regiment with career prospects and it appears Artegan must have absconded and made for the mainland, where he held up a man named James Long and robbed him of his coat and waistcoat. Curiously, the soldier then returned to the Island but, unfortunately for him, so did his victim. and they met by chance in Newport High Street. As a result, a long chase followed that ended at Niton, where the soldier was arrested. You did not at this time have to commit murder to face the gallows. Robbery on the highway and passing counterfeit coins was also a qualification. At Winchester Assizes the soldier was sentenced to hang. Not content with passing the ultimate sentence, the judge added theatre to the proceedings. He ordered that he be returned to the Isle of Wight, to be hanged opposite the main gate of the barracks. A newspaper account picks up the tale after Artegan was brought from Winchester on August 6, 1814. "The prisoner was conveyed from

The Dolphin Inn, Sea Street

Winchester in a post chaise, properly attended, and when he arrived on the Island was drawn to the place of execution, a gently rising piece of ground opposite the barrack gate, in a cart with his arms pinioned behind him. He was attended by a Roman Catholic priest.

"He arrived at the fatal spot cool and collected and engaged in earnest conversation with his spiritual attendant, who appeared to be most assiduously employed in inspiring him with hope and preparing him to meet his Creator with a confidence of his mercy to repentance. When the cart came beneath the gallows, the unfortunate man looked up to see the rope the hangman was fastening but his fortitude did not forsake him.

"Before the rope was placed around his neck, he stood up in the cart and after the priest audibly uttered his last prayer he shed a few tears, crossed himself and shook hands with the hangman and the minister.

"The cart was driven away and he died without a struggle. The public execution, involving death by slow strangulation, was held opposite the gates of what is today Albany Prison, and is the only one that we believe ever took place here.

IT'S CARISBROOKE.... AND TIME FOR TEA

by Alan Stroud

The truth is, Carisbrooke isn't what it used to be. Once upon a time people used to go out of their way to go there, but today? Well we might pass through it on the way to somewhere else but would we visit it for its own sake? Sorry Carisbrooke, not really.

But it wasn't always so. 100 years ago the village was heaving. It had its own railway station, two hotels and two working mills, Kents and Priory, both with picturesque millponds. There were trout in the Lukely Brook, a nunnery, and a castle. A 1931 tourist guide said of Carisbrooke, "The village is as charming, clean-looking and delightfully situated as any in the Island. Excursionists come in their thousands. Every other house bears the legend, Tea Parties Accommodated." The last sentence was certainly true. Carisbrooke was no slouch when it came to having a brew up. If you fainted in Carisbrooke in those days you'd almost certainly hit a tea shop on the way to the ground. They were so numerous the rattle of bone china could be heard a mile away. Even in this photograph of the ford at the bottom of Castle Street there are two tea shops to be seen. 'Mrs Fry - Teas Provided' says one sign while another, just a few feet away, announces, 'Tea Gardens – Plain Tea 6d."

It wasn't all tea at Carisbrooke, though. At the top of the High Street, opposite the Waverley, stand a pair of cottages that 100 years ago were home to the Cutters Arms public house, shown here. Kevin Mitchell in his excellent book 'Newport Pubs,' tells us that it might be one of the oldest pubs on the Island and that its former name was "The Gelders Arms." Perhaps that was on account of the number of balls held there. The name fell out of fashion in Victorian times and not long after, so did the pub. It served its last pint in 1927.

This is Castle Street in October 1925. The building in the centre distance is Millbank Cottage. In the mid-1970s the cottage stood empty and derelict but clearly it hadn't let the side down all those years ago. On the wall, in huge capital letters, could still be seen the words, 'Teas Provided.'

A SHIPWRECK WITH A CARGO OF PROBLEMS

by Brian Greening

Brighstone was transformed at five o'clock one morning in March, 1862, when the barque Cedarine was driven ashore. She had on board a crew of thirteen, plus four wives, eighteen children and one hundred and ninety-one convicts on their way back to England from Bermuda for release. A very high tide meant the ship came to within just 20 yards of the shore — and fortunately all that was required was a rope to be thrown out to her. By this means the majority of the able-bodied convicts eventually managed to get ashore with no loss of life, while the women and children and a few sick prisoners were taken off by the local life-boat. The latter were taken to Brighstone by horse and cart and put up at the local inns and other houses.

Many of the able-bodied convicts also made their way, thirstily, along the lanes to the village's two local pubs, The Five Bells and The New Inn. Landlords Edward Reynolds and James Downer must have thought all their ships had come in together, since, as the men were returning home to be released, they were in possession of their own money. Thus, there was not a problem serving meals and glasses of local ale — and soon the two establishments were overwhelmed.

On hearing there was another pub at nearby Shorwell, many of the men made their way there. Soon the scene was one of mayhem. A message was sent to Parkhurst Barracks, where Colonel Jeffery soon got his troops together to make a rapid response. But, in the minimum of three or four hours, a man can drink a lot of beer, especially if they have been in prison for seven years. The troops arrived in a heavy downpour, by which time the convicts were under the influence of the beer and several fights had broken out. Mostly they were fist fights but some were said to be in the Lancashire fashion, by kicking opponents. Soon, several horse-drawn carts, wagons and vans had been requisitioned from nearby farms and the shipwrecked men were taken to Parkhurst Prison, where they were accommodated overnight in familiar surroundings. Despite everything, it was said that, in general, all the convicts had behaved well.

The thirteen-man crew were said to be mostly men of colour, something that would have come as quite a novelty at this time to these Island villagers. In the weeks that followed, two local men were prosecuted for being in possession of government property. Apparently, on hearing the ship was in difficulty, Mr Brooke, of Grange Farm, instructed Isaac Morris and John Russell, two of his employees, to take a wagon and horses to the beach and give what assistance they could. They brought back to Brighstone the women and children and a few sick convicts to the local pub. Many of the prisoners had come ashore with distinctive blankets around them, which had the broad arrow of government convict property and were marked 'Boaz Island', one of the Bermudian Islands they had inhabited. A prisoner told the two Brighstone men that as they had no further need of the blankets, they could have them as a reward for their trouble. Later, however, on to the scene came Police Sgt Biles, a man who, according to the census, lived at Yarmouth. Sgt Biles had a nose for crime and, following reports of pilfering from the wreck, he went to the nearby Grange Farm. There, he asked Russell if he had any government property, to which he replied "Just a few blankets that had been given him by the convicts. They went to the man's beachside cottage and he was asked to show the officer the offending items.

The two farm hands made their first mistake, and maintaining they felt they had done nothing wrong did not sit easily in the officer's mind, after finding the blankets beneath nailed-down floorboards.

Bringing the lifeboat back ashore at Brighstone.

Five more were found sewn-up inside a straw mattress. This was evidence that would have gone against them in court and both men were bailed at Newport Petty Session to appear later at Winchester Assizes where, despite good references from their employer, the men were made an example of and each was given six months in prison.

Relations between the villagers of Brighstone and the police at this time must have been a little fraught. In another report, just a short time after the convict incident, another ship came ashore carrying 33,000 pineapples. The shoreline was covered for miles with the delicacy and attracted many villagers. Returning from the beach one morning, carrying a few of the seawater damaged fruit, were villagers Mrs Mary Thompson and her neighbours, Emily Cooper, Charlotte Morris and a Mrs Holbrooke.

Who should appear, however, from behind a hedge but PC Grist, who soon discovered the illicit items and charged the women with stealing wrecked goods. At their Newport court appearance, the bench decided each pineapple, even though damaged by the seawater, was worth 3d and so each of the accused was made to pay that amount, depending on the number they had on their person. Mrs Thompson either had a large family or was going to make jam, as she was fined 6/9d for the illicit fruit and 7/6d costs. Her three friends had 33 between them

The Five Bells and the New Inn, Brighstone.

and paid the same scale of fines, plus costs. PC Grist must have been a longstanding officer, as his name reappears a few years later when he charged George Shotter with being drunk and disorderly. The village man was fined 10 shillings, with 7/6d costs.

At the same court, PC Grist himself was charged with assaulting George Shotter's son, Thomas, who had gone to his father's aid when the PC apprehended him. Thomas was struck in the mouth by the policeman and knocked to the ground. Supporting evidence on Thomas Shotter's behalf was given by his drinking partner at the New Inn, William Trent, of Chilton, and the court decided the policeman had overstepped the mark and fined him 2/6d with 7/6d costs — considerably less than the man's father had to pay for being drunk.

This was not the end of the shenanigans, however, as a few days later windows in the policeman's house were smashed and upon going to investigate, he was hit in the chest by half a house brick and was then set upon by several unidentified villagers. He received cuts and bruises and said in court he had been unable to work since the incident. As a result, another local man, William Merwood, was charged with assaulting PC Grist and he received two months in prison with hard labour — underlining Brighstone being very unlike the peaceful village it is today.

by Alan Stroud

Forty years ago, Henry Hislop of Cowes, now in his eighties, was a presenter on St Mary's Hospital Radio. What a good thing he was. During his time there, Henry recorded some fascinating interviews with various locals talking about Island life in times gone by and not only did he have the good sense to record the interviews in the first place - he kept them. This month, two of Henry's interviews see the light of day after over 40 years on the shelf. The first is with someone well known to many older Cowes readers - Eric Rashley of Rashley's Stores in Park Road, Cowes who tells of a way of shopping a whole world away from today...

"I left school at the beginning of the war and went into the grocery and bakery business which my grandfather had started in 1877. We had a horse and cart that went around Cowes delivering, an old van for the outlying districts and a handcart for the local area; it's in Calbourne Mill now. In those days labour was very cheap and you had time to run about and look after people. You would go out and visit the customers, collect their order and then come back and assemble it and deliver it to them. If you were lucky, that was paid for next week. The normal way was to have credit - everybody had at least a week's credit. Some had far more than that and you were lucky if you got squared up!

"There were no washing machines in those days and Monday morning was wash day for everybody so because you didn't see very many faces that was our 'wrapping-up day.' We would wrap up a week's supply of tea, sugar, dried fruit and candles. We had our own brand of tea. It came from Brooke Bond but it had our wrapper around it. Candles were big business in those days. Lots of houses only had gas lighting and we would sell a tremendous amount in winter time. Fats were all loose. You had slabs of butter, margarine and lard, all on marble slabs, and that was weighed up as the customers wanted. Very few shops had refrigeration then, so Saturday nights, particularly in hot weather, you had to get rid of all your bacon and perishable stuff so there were 'Saturday night bargains'. We used to open until nine o'clock Saturday nights and people would come along just before closing time and they knew they'd get a bargain because you had to get rid of the stuff. It was no good keeping it .... "

Shop and bakery staff in the bakehouse at Rashley's in 1971. Third from left, Bert Symons, fourth from left, Eric Rashley and next to him, roundsman Edgar Read, and then Doug Rashley.

Henry also interviewed Les Shirlaw, born in Porchfield just over 100 years ago (a faggot, by the way, is a bundle of sticks bound together). "We had a post office combined with a bakery where old Mr Bennett made his own bread. He baked with faggots out of Bunts Hill copse; the forecourt of the shop used to be just one heap of them. They were made by old Herbert Ford who lived in a cottage in the churchyard. He could make a faggot and twist it round and tie it up while I'm saying it. Absolutely perfect.

"One night Herbert was in the Sportsman's Rest and he was sitting at the end of the counter in his usual chair with his old cherry-pipe in his mouth, his head slumped down and his beard halfway down to his waist. They drew Herbert off a pint and slid it up the counter and said, "Come on Herbert, have a drink." But Herbert didn't move. He'd died. And his pipe was still in his mouth. They thought, 'Well, we'd better get him back to his cottage,' which was just past the brook, so they took the farm gate off, opposite the pub, and carried him on that. When they got to the gate to go into his garden, the wide farm gate wouldn't go through so they tilted it a bit and tipped Herbert off into the stinging nettles and he went in the brook!

"Postman Brown delivered our letters on his bicycle. There was a blacksmith, Mr Heal, at Locks Green; his son was Charlie Heal in the gun shop at Newport. Most people kept pigs and chickens and my uncle used to go round and kill pigs for them. Mr Neat came round with his horse and cart with a big tank of oil at the back; he sold brushes and everything. You could go to any farm and get milk, those days. I used to stand at the Homestead, just up the road from the Sportsman's, and see it milked out and tipped into my can straight from the cow…"

Herbert Ford wasn't the only one to breathe his last at the Sportsman's Rest. Fast forward to 1966 and this *County Press* cutting ….

"**THIRSTY ADDER MEETS ITS DOOM** — Patrons always get a friendly welcome at the Sportsman's Rest but the exception proves the rule. On Monday landlady, Mrs. Jill Tilbury, had a shock when she saw the first customer of the morning — an adder. By way of introduction the visitor flung back its head and hissed. Mrs Tilbury called for her husband, who, armed with a mallet, called a hasty "Time, gentlemen, please" for the adder. With the introductions complete, Mr. Tilbury transferred the adder to a large jar — evidence for any friends who might otherwise have doubted the story."

The Sportsmans Rest during World War I. The pub's name has been painted over to confuse any thirsty Germans who might have turned up. Photo from 'The Book of Porchfield' by kind permission of Keir Foss.

by Brian Greening

In recent years, the actions of some associated with the banking world have hit the headlines, again reiterating that in life little changes. Research of Island archives shines a light on two directors of a Newport bank in 1844 who fraudulently siphoned off over £130,000, equivalent today to around £15 million. They were Messrs Blachford and Roe, two ex-mayor's of Newport. The former was a relative of the once-owner of Osborne House, before Queen Victoria acquired it, the latter the son-in-law of Sir Richard Bassett, a man who was mayor himself of Newport on ten occasions. They were eventually prosecuted and made to resign as directors of the bank but beyond the disgrace and shame this appeared their only punishment.

Not so lucky nine years later was William Wheeler Yelf, the proprietor of a printing business in Holyrood Street. One Saturday morning in April, 1853, rumours circulated Newport, telling of a confession that had been made

THE HOUSE

THE first mention of Holyrood Street is to be found in the Unpublished Court Rolls of 1406 in the Public Record Office where it appears as *Holirodestret* and later as *Holirodestrete* in the Augmentation Office Proceedings in 1415. Various spellings occur over the years but it appears as Holyroodstreet in the Rentals and Surveys of the Public Record Office of 1608. It is delineated in John Speed's Map of 1611 but here the spelling is *Holy rodde st.*

The land in Holyrood Street was among that sold by the Corporation in 1813, formerly being held by the burgesses to whom it had originally been given by Isabella de Fortibus, Countess of Devon and Lady of the Island who granted the borough its second charter in the reign of Edward I. The first charter was granted by Richard de Redvers the Third in the reign of Henry II and the final royal charter of Charles II in 1684 completed a series of sixteen granted over five centuries.

to two directors of the Isle of Wight Savings Bank. The evil tidings spread like wildfire, helped by the fact that it was Newport's Saturday market day, and nearly every parish on the Island had a representative in town.

The notice read:

> ## Isle of Wight Savings Bank.
> The trustees and directors regret to be under the necessity of informing the public that, in consequence of a defalcation in the actuary's accounts, the bank is for the present closed. Every necessary information will be communicated and when the accounts are investigated the directors confidently trust the loss will not exceed two to three shillings in the pound.

The list of directors of the bank read like an Isle of Wight Who's Who. Included were such names as Barrington, Oglander, George Ward, of Northwood, Michael Hoy and George Player, as well as church representatives from every Island parish. Also to be affected were many of the working class who used the bank to save from their meagre wages for their funerals. It was later found that over a period of eight years the employee, William Wheeler Yelf, had embezzled more than £8,000, considerably less than the two other crooks but still equivalent today to around £1million pounds.

Yelf was brought before the magistrates at Newport and bank trustee George Kirkpatrick told the court that on Saturday morning, he had received the following letter:

Sir,

An insupportable and daily increasing weight of anguish compels me at length to reveal a secret that has destroyed my health and is, I feel, cutting short my days. For years, the fallacious hope of being able by some means to retrieve my character and repair the wrong, induced me, in spite of my better judgment, to maintain a guilty silence which I dare no longer continue. The awful fact is the unbounded confidence placed in me was, many years ago, in a moment of sudden and great pecuniary embarrassment, abused and the boundaries of truth and honesty, once broken through, I was miserably led, step by step, on the downward path to ruin.

I now feel the only thing I can do is by a disclosure to prevent the evil spreading further and to beg of you and the other trustees to take possession of all I have on behalf of the sufferers and I do voluntarily place myself in the hands of the trustees to receive that punishment I deserve as the only means I have left to prove my sincere repentance of the crimes I have committed. It will be the more necessary for prompt and immediate action as I fear having a distraint from the Crown which your possession may prevent.

Before you receive this I shall have broken the terrible secret to my unfortunate and innocent wife and son and may God support them under the trial. I sincerely hope they will experience that merciful consideration and pity from your hands and the hands of the trustees which I dare not hope for and do not deserve.

I am, sir, your unfaithful but truly penitent servant,
William Wheeler Yelf.

Yelf was remanded in custody for trial at Winchester Assizes. While awaiting trial, an advertisement appeared in the local newspapers for the sale of his effects that included more than two tons of valuable printing types, inking tables, three Albion presses, a bookbinder's press, masses of general stationery and artifacts as well as a library of 600 books and a pair of globes. In fact, all his worldly wealth was there including household furniture, linen, glass and china. He was later convicted at Winchester Assizes and, despite a plea for leniency by his solicitor, he was sentenced to transportation for the rest of his natural life. The last reference to him was in March of the following year, when a three-line entry in the local newspaper said simply:

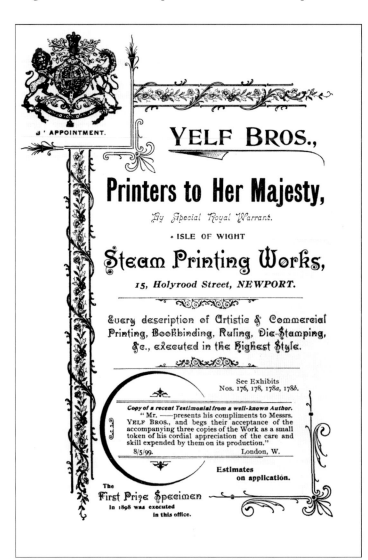

"William Wheeler Yelf, the actuary and great defaulter of the IW Savings Bank, died yesterday in Millbank Prison, London. He had been awaiting transportation to a penal colony."

The sale of all Yelf's worldly goods however never took place and the business flourished for more than another 100 years. There is surmise that influential creditors decided it was more beneficial to keep the business going and helped his son, William Richard, in that cause. It would, after all, help them to recover some of their losses.

The fate of the two other well-connected bank directors, Blachford and Roe, who ten years earlier had embezzled twelve times the money of Yelf, remains undocumented. While Yelf died a broken man, rank, status, membership of the right societies and influential friends appeared to have been their saviours.

Illustrations taken from the book, *Printers' Pride, the House of Yelf at Newport, IW, 1816-1966.*

MR. MILLIDGE - THE CHEMIST WITH THE CAMERA.

by Alan Stroud

In 1832, 21-year-old William Millidge left his home in Alverstoke near Gosport and came to the Island to open a chemist's shop at 47 High Street, Newport. It was a good move. Nearly 150 years later "Millidge, The Chemist" was still trading from the very same premises when it finally closed in 1973. In his eighties, Mike Millidge of Newport is William's great-great-grandson and he had the good sense to hold on to memorabilia from the family business, including a collection of glass negatives taken at the turn of the last century by his grandfather Philip Millidge. Although he never actually worked in the business, Mike remembers his grandfather and the shop very well…. "I can remember when I was about four, just before the war, going upstairs in the shop and sitting in the bay window to watch the carnival. They came by with poles with long stockings on to catch money in, because lots of shop owners lived above the shop then, and I remember being given some pennies to drop into this sock from the window.

"When I was at school, about 10 or 11, we found a recipe for gunpowder. So I went to my grandfather in the shop and asked him for some of the chemicals and he wrapped them up in some little paper packets for me. I didn't even pay him for it! He didn't ask what I wanted it for but I expect he worked it out. Then I made my own charcoal and ground it all up! It didn't go as well as I thought it might do but it did go off with a flash!

"I can remember getting medicines from there. If I had a cold I immediately went down to my grandfather. You didn't go to the doctor. You went to my grandfather and he would mix up a tonic - Millidge's cough mixture was the thing! There was a tonic he used to mix up if I had a stomach upset. It was rhubarb and soda in a tiny little bottle which I hated because it tasted awful. It was brown in colour, a mixture of bicarbonate of soda, I think, and

Situated opposite today's Waterstones, 47 High Street was home to Millidge & Son from 1832 to 1973.

rhubarb extract. A teaspoon was the dose. I was always told if it didn't taste nice it was doing you good! I remember there were scales in the shop because I used to be taken in there to be weighed when I was a baby. I think all the chemists did it.

"My grandfather eventually sold the business. None of his sons were that much interested, so the business passed out of the family in 1946, when my grandfather was in his seventies but it carried on trading under the name Millidge."

Philip Millidge, who died in 1972, left behind a treasure trove of nearly 100 glass plate negatives, mainly taken between 1900 and the mid 1920s. Many of them are still in their original envelopes complete with Mr Millidge's hand-written titles. Obviously a meticulous man, he has written not only the location of each photograph and the date, but even the day of the week! The bulk of the plates are of locations in and around Newport and Carisbrooke and date from 1905 to the mid 1920s. They range from Newport High Street to rural scenes on the River Medina. There are photographs of Whitepit Lane and Petticoat Lane when they both really were lanes, unrecognisable scenes across fields of crops at Shide that became today's Medina Avenue and surrounding roads, and wonderful photographs of St Cross, Westminster Lane and Pan Farm.

Philip Millidge took all his photographs using a bulky glass plate camera made from wood and brass. Cheap pocket-sized Kodak roll-film cameras were around by this time but serious photographers preferred plate cameras because of their much higher quality. The downside was lugging it from place to place.

There was no such thing as an instant snap in those days. The camera had to be mounted on its wooden tripod, a struggle at the best of times, and then the glass plates were loaded into the camera one at a time, in a light proof carrier, and then exposed. There were no digital settings to work out the exposure - just an educated guess. Then it was back to the darkroom to develop the plates. It was a lot of work and a labour of love. Thanks to Mr. Millidge's grandson Mike, it was all worthwhile.

Pan Bridge, looking towards South Street, one sleepy afternoon in July 1905, photographed by Philip Millidge (inset). He is stood outside what today is car park for the shops and cinema complex. The row of cottages on the right-hand side are in lower Pyle Street. Not a single building in this picture exists today.

LAST TRAIN TO A CARING PAST

by Brian Greening

Two government decisions of tremendous importance taken during my younger days affected the life of our Island. One was the cutting of a major slice of the Island rail network, the other the closure of Whitecroft Hospital. The connection between the two? The enjoyment I derived from being able to use both facilities.

The Newport to Ryde railway line ran along the bottom of our garden at the Fairlee Road home where I grew up. There was no need for a clock in the house, as my father knew that at thirty-five minutes past the hour the train came down from Whippingham and into Newport. As soon as it reached Newport, another left in the opposite direction on the way to Ryde so we knew it was time for him to set off for work. I would play in a school football team against schools across the Island and what great excitement there was on a Saturday morning when I met all my team mates at Newport Railway Station and got on the train for, say Freshwater. Over the bridge at Hunnyhill, on through Carisbrooke and Calbourne, all the time looking at the wonderful scenery. When in short trousers, I would stand on Snooks Hill and watch the train leave Newport Station and come toward me, to disappear, briefly into the

A train from Ryde, on its way to Cowes, has just passed through the Fairlee tunnel and crosses the viaduct across the Medina as it pulls into Newport station.

tunnel before emerging in a cloud of steam in the cutting beside Victoria Road. At carnival time, my mother would enter my twin sisters in processions all over the Island, always with a decorated tableau on wheels. Too big for the bus, the guards van came to her rescue, especially when entering East Cowes, Sandown or Ryde carnivals.

How would the impatient motorists of today cope with the delay in completing their journey when the level crossing gates were across the road at places such as Shide, Blackwater and Horringford? When the time came for the very last train to leave Newport station en-route to Ryde, I went with my father and eldest son up to the bridge near Halberry Lane. Three generations of the Greening family witnessed that historic event that morning.

Strangely enough, I only recently found that Dr. Beeching, who took all the blame for our rail closures, simply wrote a report for the Conservative government in 1963. They lost power shortly afterwards and it was the Labour party, via Harold Wilson and Barbara Castle, who carried out Beeching's recommendations in 1966. As Michael Caine might say. "Not a lot of people know that."

A Freshwater-bound train sits in the siding at Newport Station

The building of Whitecroft Hospital was one of the first tasks undertaken by the newly established IW County Council when it was formed in 1890. Within four years, a site had been found, one fortunately with enough sand and clay to make six million bricks and enough water to service a small town. But the chairman of the then County Council, the Rt Hon Gough Calthorpe, declined to lay a foundation stone. He felt it was the type of institution that should be kept in the background and no ceremony as such should be undertaken as it might give the place publicity. Victorian values methinks.

Whitecroft Hospital

As the years rolled by public opinion was that they could not have found a better site. It was set in spacious grounds, just three miles from Newport, available to both buses and trains but at a place that provided the most tranquil of settings for people who were in need of a bit of peace, quiet and rest. The social side of the hospital was encouraged and developed and, in the late 1950s I was able to take advantage of some of those facilities, playing football and cricket for the hospital on their sports ground that is known as Hungry Hill.

Patients were encouraged to participate in hospital events and the cricket team invariably had a couple in it, and some, like Bill Brewer entered in the local carnivals each year, Bill always depicting himself as Charlie Chaplin.

Years earlier, the highlight of the football calendar was the local derby between Chillerton and a team representing Whitecroft. One of the star players for the Asylum team was the Vicar of Gatcombe, the Rev. Wayet, who by all accounts, was quite skilful and fast. Thus, it fell to Harold Gerrett, a man who lived more than ninety years in Chillerton, to mark the reverend gentleman. If descriptions of the methods adopted by Harold are true, he might have found difficulty later to being admitted through the pearly gates. Harold was a real 'son of the soil' and he told me how in his youth he asked a young nurse from Whitecroft out and they embarked on a long walk over the downs. His plan was to eventually take her into the bus shelter at Gatcombe. When they reached this spot, she declined with the words: "My mother said if I was ever to go out with a boy, I was to keep walking." Sounder advice has never been given.

Many of the patients became good friends and I particularly remember Ron Maynard, a man who would always bring the tea urn and refreshments up to the sports ground from the main hospital. Whitecroft was home to Ron, a man who became traumatised following service in aircraft during the Second World War. The staff were a tremendous group and included Bruce Charman, the hospital administrator, Jimmy Carr, who was in charge of occupational therapy, and nurses such as Bernard Ellis and Richard Benfield. All four played in the cricket team.

Then the time came to close the place and introduce something called 'Care in the Community.' Years later I would see Ron walking around the town. He always seemed quite lonely. From having all his friends around him at Whitecroft, he was placed into something that was like bed and breakfast. It may have

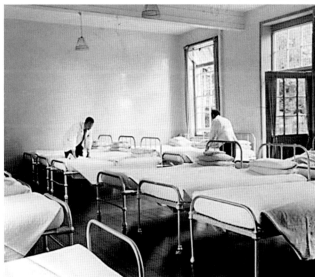
A ward in Whitecroft Hospital

worked out cheaper for the County council but Ron had lost what had been his home for the past twenty-five years. He died in 1994, aged just 71, but I do not believe he died a happy man.

by Alan Stroud

Well not quite - but almost. In 2015, *Island Story* took a look at those far off, heady days when semi-nudists and German spies stalked the land, and sex reared its ugly head in Sandown Library of all places. In 1937, under the headline "Semi-Nudists Walking in the Streets of Sandown and Shanklin" the *County Press* reported, "A council meeting was held to discuss what was described as the semi-nude condition of some visitors walking in the streets of Sandown and Shanklin. Mr. W. Russell said he objected to the condition in which men and women were walking about the towns. Some hairy men with a lot of whiskers lead one to imagine he was at the Zoo. It was really disgusting... They should pass some byelaw to keep these people out of the streets. People don't know how to behave themselves. They try to be as rude as they can...It would be unfortunate if it went forth to the

Sandown High Street; the home of hairy men with whiskers.

world that Sandown and Shanklin was full of indecent people." .... Perish the thought.

"Death Sentence on Sandown Woman Convicted of Treason. " This strange but true headline appeared in 1940 when Dorothy O'Grady, a Sandown housewife, was found guilty of being a German spy - although today most agree that she was nothing more than an eccentric fantasist with a taste for excitement. During the war, Sandown, like much of the Island, was dotted with military installations in areas that were out of bounds to the public. Dorothy was arrested in one such area near searchlights at Yaverland. She had made detailed sketches of gun batteries, she admitted cutting telephone lines between installations and she was wearing a swastika badge under her lapel but at her trial, held in secret, there was no evidence that she had ever passed any of this information on. She had no radio, no understanding of codes and had never been abroad, let alone to Germany. Nevertheless she was found guilty and sentenced to death by hanging and was placed in the condemned suite in Holloway prison until her execution three weeks later. An appeal was immediately launched and eventually the death sentence was commuted to 14 years in jail. When the trial notes were declassified in 1995 it became clear just how close Dorothy had come to losing her life. The Director Of Public Prosecutions had written to the Home Office during the appeal, "I think that the sentence of death ought to go forward. If this woman is reprieved the knowledge would go to the public and the German intelligence service and serve as an encouragement to female spies." Dorothy spent the next ten years in jail and was released in 1950, returning to the Island to live. She died at Lake in 1985, aged 87, still protesting her innocence, describing herself as a daydreamer with an overactive imagination. She gave several interviews before she died, declaring in one, "Looking back, I realise I must have been suffering from some sort of kink. What I did in wartime was stupid and I brought the punishment on myself. I know people will always think of me as a spy but I never was. I was just a very silly woman who got the punishment she deserved."

For the most part, Dorothy's wartime activities still remain a mystery. In 1995 the then MP for the Island, Barry Field, was asked to take part in a campaign for a posthumous pardon for Mrs O'Grady. He agreed until he was given sight of the still secret case papers when he declared "I am staggered by the treachery this woman sank to. Far from being a simple seaside landlady, she was a highly skilled agent who produced masterpieces of defence systems for the Third Reich. She could have altered the course of the war."

For over 60 years the contents of the Home Office file on Mrs O'Grady remained an official secret. The file was eventually declassified in 2006 only to be removed from public view a few weeks later "in the conduct of official business." Six months later, when National Archives requested the return of the file, the Home Office said it could no longer be traced. Since then inquiries to the Public Records Office as to its whereabouts have gone unanswered.

Moving on, it's the summer of 1946 and on the Sandown beaches where Dorothy once strode, dreaming of the Fatherland, a holidaymaker was helping his little girl make sandcastles when he saw what looked like a bicycle pedal poking out from the sand. He was right. Unbelievably, it was a complete 'penny-farthing' bicycle. It was minus its tyres, but otherwise in fairly good order after at least 60 years in the sand. It was put on display outside Hoopers beach ticket office where it became a popular attraction for some years.

Bathing machines on Sandown beach c. 1910

Meanwhile, by 1965 the genie of sexual liberation had begun to pop out of the bottle – On the Island, efforts were made to put the cork back in. Sandown and Shanklin's library committee had received a complaint from a Mrs Longmate of Shanklin, describing the book "A Singular Man," by J.P. Donleavy as "unsuitable for young people." The chairman of the committee, Mr. Holmes, dutifully sat down to read the book, the *County Press* reporting, "He said if it was withdrawn the committee would have to take most of the other books off the shelves. The vice-chairman, Mr. Barber, disagreed and said the book had no story and was a series of descriptions of sexual behaviour. Miss M. Wright (librarian) said there had been a good demand for the book, mainly from the "young moderns." It was agreed to remove the book."

Sandown pier in a previous life. Jim Davidson once appeared here - but it's not all bad news - so did Frankie Howerd, Norman Wisdom and Jimmy Tarbuck.

by Brian Greening

Shopping and life in general today has become so impersonal. Phone up your gas or electricity supplier to query your bill and you are asked to choose from one of up to eight options. You can be kept waiting for ages while all the time being told your call is important and an operator will be with you shortly. It would help if the music they played was from the sixties - Handel's water music has its limits. At such time always make sure you have a razor handy as by the time they do answer we men will need a shave, and the ladies will have time to sandpaper their legs.

Try to buy something with a credit card and they will need to know your name, address, post code, the type of card, the expiry date, the secret three numbers on the back and, recently, I was asked for my inside leg

Whitchers, 'The Wight Mans Clothiers' at the junction of High Street and Holyrood Street

measurement. I admit though I got that number out of a telephone box. I would not have minded, but all I was buying was a second-hand copy of Lady Chatterley's Lover. More than one hundred years ago, before Newport's town centre was a proliferation of coffee shops, charity shops, hairdressers, estate agents and those very impersonal supermarkets, we had businesses that had been in the town for well over one hundred years.

Any Newport resident of fifty years ago will remember the names that read a little like the England cricket team. Alderslades, Snellgroves, Jukes, Whitchers, Wadham's, Guys, Sheaths, Wray's, Jordan and Stanley, and those two wonderful veterans, Upward and Rich. One reason for their success was the personal services they all offered. Another thing I recall was these premises all had an individual aroma. In Pyle Street today there is a coffee shop that in my youth was S. J. Guys, where I would buy seven pounds of mixed corn to feed the chickens my father kept. The smell here came from the various open sacks around the shop, each carrying meal, corn, mixed bran, dog biscuits and dried peas, etc. I remember the last item, because we bought them to fire from our pea shooters.

This shop went back to 1867 when Samuel Guy bought the premises and set up as a corn merchant. The building is believed to date back as far as 1768, when it was a public house known as the Star and Garter. Samuel Guy had married into another old-established Newport family when he wed, believe it or not, Jane Aderslade, whose family were decorator's merchants.

Reputed to be the oldest provision merchant in England at one time was the firm of Upward and Rich, which was a wholesale grocer with premises in Pyle Street, almost opposite Guy's shop. It is believed to have been founded on the same site in 1650, owned by John Upward. Later, Mr G. Rich became a partner. Even though he died in 1921, a Miss Rich continued to be involved in the company as a director for many years. There was a time, around 1890, when the firm was taken to court to abate the terrible smell given off by its candle production. This is not surprising, since the candles were made from the boiled-up waste, blood and offal thrown away by the local slaughter houses, many of these being in Scarrott's Lane.

Samuel Jordan came to Newport in 1869 and went into business with Mr Stanley and thus was formed the very successful business of Jordan and Stanley, grocers and provision merchants. Charles Wadham started a business in Newport in 1860 and, after originally having premises in Lower High Street, purchased property in 1873 in St

Wadhams furniture store, St James Square.

James's Square that also had a frontage in the High Street. They were the Island furnishers where many newlyweds went to buy their first bed, chest of drawers and front room carpet.

Wray and Sons had shops all over the Island and at least three in Newport. At the time of their closure in 1987, this business was being run by brothers Vivian, Peter and Leslie, plus one of their cousins. Two other brothers, Max and Edward, had already taken early retirement. Here, cheese was cut into shape from a large block with a wire and still having on it the tough rind. Sugar was weighed and emptied into blue bags. Biscuits were not pre-packaged but lay in glass-top tins. Wray's shops had an indescribable mixture of smells. Fresh-cut bacon, cheese, currants and raisins and mixed peal, mixed up with the aroma of freshly ground coffee. Had the Wray family found the secret of bottling that smell, they would all have retired early as millionaires.

In none of these old shops did you have to stand in a queue with ten other people while six checkouts positions remain unmanned. None of the old shops encouraged you to contribute to the number of unemployed by scanning your own shopping whilst shop assistants wandered aimlessly around with clipboards. I was asked recently to wait for assistance as I tried to purchase my single bottle of beer because the machine didn't know whether I was 17 or 79. When the assistant arrived she asked for some identification. In none of the old shops

Wray's shop at the top of Newport High Street.

was I reduced to telling a piece of metal to —— off when an automated voice told me to "replace the item in the bag" as I walked out into the car park leaving my items behind. Is it any wonder my old mate Keith Newbery called me Grumpy?

As we get older, we seem to look back with great fondness to the days of our youth. Were they better times to live through? Well, apart from the hazard of contracting typhoid and rickets and having an outside loo, I can only put forth my own opinion — an emphatic "Yes."

VICTORIA – QUEEN OF ENGLAND AND HOUSEWIFE OF EAST COWES

by Alan Stroud

These three photos of the Queen's 1897 Jubilee celebrations at Newport are notable for a couple of reasons – firstly, they are of the same event, taken within minutes of each other, and secondly, the Queen is smiling.

Island residents were used to the sight of their monarch as she had lived at Osborne House since the early 1840s. Never owned by the state, it was the personal property of the Queen, bought with her own money; a private home where she could do what she liked when she liked. Writing to an uncle she said: "You will be pleased to hear that we have purchased Osborne; it is so nice to have a quiet place of one's own, free from the charming Departments who are the plague of one's life." Balmoral, in the Scottish Highlands, was another private purchase, deliberately aimed at dissuading her Ministers from turning up at her door unannounced.

For the next fifty years the two homes provided the Queen with an escape from the affairs of state. After Albert died, leaving her a widow at 42, she was shattered, and withdrew from public life. Her virtual disappearance and her appointment of John Brown as manservant saw her popularity plummet but by the time of her 1897 Jubilee, Brown was dead, the Queen was rehabilitated, and now she could do no wrong.

The Island saw a long series of Jubilee celebrations. "After tea, drove to Newport through the beautifully decorated streets. At the Square we stopped in a front of a platform on which stood the Mayor & Corporation. We left amidst great cheering." The *County Press* noted, "The Queen was all smiles and looked in perfect health."

The same moment as opposite, but from a different vantage point.

By this time Island residents had grown used to the sight of their Queen out and about on Island roads. On February 14th, 1891, under the headline "The Queen and The Blind Man," the *County Press* reported : "The Queen drove into Newport on Monday, and when returning, Her Majesty's attention was arrested by a blind man, who, told by a boy who was leading him that the Queen was coming, had drawn up by the side of Fairlee Road and stood with bared head as the Queen passed. After a short distance the Royal carriage stopped, and a messenger came back to the blind man and placed a gift of money in his hand 'from the Queen'.

On New Year's Day, 1901, the Queen wrote in her diary, "I am feeling so weak and unwell that I enter upon it sadly." Three weeks later, on Tuesday, January 22nd, at half past six in the evening, the Queen died in her bedroom at Osborne in the arms of her grandson, the Kaiser. Her son Edward, now King, closed her eyes, and the announcement of her death was posted at the gates of Osborne House where large crowds had gathered.

Victoria was the first monarch whose death was reported electronically. Local boys had been recruited by Fleet Street reporters to race down to East Cowes post office on their bicycles, with a bonus for the first one to reach the telegraph counter where forty extra staff had been drafted in to work through the night. In a matter of minutes the news of the Queen's death was telegraphed to London and the Empire.

The following day, the Queen's body was viewed by the household and servants, "Yesterday, 300 of the tenants, with their wives and families, were permitted to pass through the room in which the body is lying. There lay their beloved Queen, beautiful in her long sleep. With calm and placid face, wearing her widow's cap, with her hands crossed in perfect repose," wrote the *County Press*.

A triple-shell coffin was prepared for the Queen. Her body was placed in the inner shell, made from oak from the Osborne estate, and this was then placed inside a mahogany, lead-lined, outer shell, but before any of this could be done, there were secret matters to be seen to. The Queen's dresser, Mrs. Tuck, took Sir James Reid, the Queen's doctor, aside and produced a secret note that had been given to her by the Queen three years before. The Queen, who always enjoyed a good funeral, had left a handwritten note detailing 'very minute instructions' as to the actions to be taken after her death. It included details of items to be placed in her coffin, 'some of which, none of her family were to see'. The faithful Doctor Reid, who had attended the Queen for twenty years (but had never

The same moment photographed from Lower St James Street. The Queen can just be made out in her carriage.

been allowed to examine her!) followed her instructions to the letter. "I helped Mrs Tuck put a satin dressing gown on the Queen. We cut her hair and rearranged the flowers, put a layer of charcoal on the floor of the coffin and then the Kaiser, King Edward and myself, lifted the Queen's body into it." When the doctor was finally alone, he carried out the Queen's last instructions. He placed in the coffin Albert's dressing gown, the Queen's wedding veil, a sprig of Balmoral heather, a cast of Albert's hands, numerous photographs and pieces of jewellery.

Finally, Doctor Reid placed a bunch of flowers in the Queen's hands. They were strategically placed to conceal the fact that in her left hand the Queen held a photograph of John Brown.

THE MUSIC THEY HAVEN'T MADE SINCE I WAS A BOY.......

by Brian Greening

One of my earlier memories was of lying in bed and listening to my father as he busied himself downstairs first thing in the morning. I would hear him as he shoveled the ashes left from the previous day's fire into a small bucket and then proceed to light the new fire for that day. Until the fire was lit, the dining room was always quite cold. Soon I would smell the bacon, eggs and fried bread being cooked and this was the signal for me to wander downstairs. Each morning at 6-30 there would be thirty minutes of music on the radio and my father was never happier than when that thirty minutes of music was played by 'Troise and his Banjoliers', the leader being an Italian gentleman who latterly formed his own group of nineteen musicians. They all initially played the mandolin but later changed to the much louder banjos. This group was a household favourite up until around 1957, when their leader died.

Our elders usually impart good advice to their children and one I recall passed down to me by my father was, "If you are going out, (usually meaning on the bus to the beach) always ensure you have money in your pocket and take some toilet paper with you." With the way they are closing public toilets today that advice has stood the test of time. Another saying I recall was handed down by my mentor, Bert Day, when I was serving my apprenticeship in the shipyard. If Bert did not think highly of an individual he would say, "That man has the brains of three high court judges," and I immediately understood the man was not that bright.

I was reminded of the music of my youth one evening when enjoying a quiet pint in a Newport ale house, and a friend of mine, who was the DJ for the evening, told me it was a 'music of the Fifties' night. I sat there and listened to the songs that I was weaned on that included such wonderful lyrics as, "Does Your Chewing Gum Lose its Flavour on the Bedpost Overnight?" I listened too to Johnny Duncan and the Bluegrass Boys, Frankie Valli, Fats Domino, the Platters, Johnny Ray, Johnny Cash and Gene Vincent. In the mid-Fifties I used to meet up with a few friends on a Saturday morning and head for Murdoch's music shop, by the Guildhall. There, all the popular records of the day could be purchased but not before you had been permitted to listen to some on headphones inside a small booth.

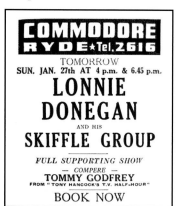

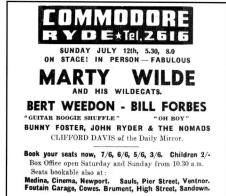

It was in the late fifties that I went to the Commodore at Ryde and saw Tommy Steele, Marty Wilde and Lonnie Donegan. This was also around the time I sat in the Medina cinema in Newport one Sunday evening and saw my school pal, Terry Perkins, win a talent contest. The rest is history. Terry soon changed his name to Craig Douglas and embarked on a lifetime in the music industry. In 1959 he topped the music charts with his version of 'Only Sixteen' and topped the bill on the Beatles first major stage show. Craig's early years were spent living in Prospect Road, part of a family that had three sets of twins, his twin being brother Tony. On leaving school he became a milkman. In all the years that I have known him Craig has changed little, still remaining in my eyes the cheeky, smiling chap who scored the winning goal in a school cup final at Church Litten at the age of thirteen, for Barton against Ryde.

Yesteryear exam

Answer all the questions. You have 30 minutes. No talking. No referring to notes or any modern aid.

● **Why are the following dates important in our country's history?**
1605, 1620, 1660, 1720, 1757, 1805, 1815 and 1840.
(As a clue, one of the dates was when the Pilgrim Fathers set sail for America in the Mayflower).
● **In the Easter English exam for the same year, the pupils were asked for the following:**
1. Name ten poems you have learnt and give the names of the authors.
2. Give six of the finest descriptive phrases you have met up with in your studies.
3. How do poets make their work so attractive that we love to read them? Give illustration.

Answers at bottom of page

At a certain time each year we see pictures of students finding out how well they have done in exams and it is nice to see the pleasure they get on finding their efforts have been worthwhile. It got me thinking about the schooldays of old, when many left at 14 and went out to find a full-time job, something today's school leavers sadly might not find until they have passed their 21st birthday. I recently discovered some exam papers given to boys aged 12 to 13 at my old school at Barton in 1923. Here are a couple of the questions :

This is not to criticize the teaching of today, as I am not familiar with it, but simply to demonstrate the level of education that was expected in those days. I admit that without Wikipedia and a computer I might struggle to supply all the answers. In those days, all the boys could do was visit the Seely library.

The exam took me back to another story that was alleged to have taken place in the village school at Chillerton but could have been anywhere. Each Friday, the local vicar would come in and take the children for an hour's Bible reading. One day he noticed a boy at the back was not paying attention, so he called to him, saying: "You boy, read on." The poor lad he picked on was unable to read or write, which was why he always hid at the back, so some quick thinking was needed. "Where from, Sir," he asked. "From where it says and Jesus rode into Jerusalem," said the vicar. The quick thinking lad retorted at once: "And Jesus rode into Jerusalem and climbed up a tree." He had to stay behind after school that day.

The other story was one I told Keith Newbery some years ago and he recorded it in his column. It told of how each Friday in the early 1950s the school secretary at Barton school would go around to each class and hand the teachers their weekly pay packet. On one occasion, after she had left the room, one of the boys asked the teacher what was in the envelope Miss had given him. "That is my wages, boy," came the reply. After a suitable pause, the boy inquired further: "Where do you work then, sir?"

Barton School in 1938 - The days before 'Mrs. Thatcher the Milk Snatcher'. In this photo are Maurice Hamilton, Doreen and John Orr, Phyliss and John Day, John and June Orchard, Nancy Smith, John and Joyce Cant ,Wyn, and John Woodford., Aubrey and Audrey Odell, Thelma and Avril Newnham, Brian and Leo Powell, Calvert, Rodney Hatcher, Ken Lillywhite, Gerald Attrill, Vic Jervis, Marion Palmer, Doris Brennan, John French, Dave Croton and Edgar Luter.

Exam answers : 1605, The Gunpowder Plot. 1620, Mayflower departed. 1660, Restoration. 1720, South Sea Bubble financial crash. 1805, Battle of Trafalgar. 1815, Battle of Waterloo. 1840, Penny post introduced.

THE DAY NEWPORT DISAPPEARED UNDERWATER

by Alan Stroud

The worst ever flood to hit the Island in living memory came on the Saturday morning of October 1st, 1960. Newport suffered the most and much of the town disappeared under several feet of water for several hours when millions of gallons of rainwater coming down from the hills met a high spring tide coming up the River Medina at exactly the same time. Unable to cope, the River Medina spectacularly burst its banks and eventually flooded Newport High Street.

The previous night there had been a freak cloudburst in the small hours and by daybreak an estimated 500 million gallons of rainwater was making its way from the surrounding hills down into Newport by fast-flowing stream and river. Unfortunately, at that exact moment a high spring tide was making its way in the opposite direction – up the River Medina. The two bodies of water met in the harbour and in a matter of minutes the sea level rose nearly three feet and the streets around Coppins Bridge disappeared under water in the worst flooding in living memory. Such was the volume of water that at Shide, where the river flow was usually six cubic feet a second, the recording equipment showed a flow of over 150 cu.ft. at one point. Shortly after, the equipment was overwhelmed and the needle ran off the chart. The flood was as short lived as it was devastating. With the turn of the tide there was a rapid fall in water levels and by two o'clock in the afternoon the waters had completely receded. Blame was variously attached to narrow bridges and culverts, inadequate sluice gates, and ancient and disused mill wheels on both the Medina and Lukely streams but it was generally agreed that the flood had not been preventable.

The events of those few hours were to have a lasting effect on Newport. In fear of a repeat occurrence, the Council and Water Board decided that the river should be 'canalised' - an ugly word for what some would say was an ugly end result. For hundreds of years the picturesque Medina had made its unspoilt way through the town centre but the canalisation brought all that to an end. The pretty grass slopes leading to the waters' edge were replaced by the stark and unimaginative concrete riverbanks which are still with us today. The end result is that apart from the excellent Town Gate Pond redevelopment, a pretty river that could be a major feature for Newport passes through the town largely hidden from view - a lost asset awaiting rediscovery.

In 2016 I recorded an interview with Mike Millidge of Newport, then in his early eighties. Mike worked for Mews and its successors for over forty years, in the brewery on the two acre site where St Cross Court and Lidl now stand. He vividly remembers being involved in the 1960 flood : "Yes. I went down and spent time sorting stuff out and getting tobacco out of the tobacco store. The building at the bottom of Hunny Hill, where the side came out of, that was the mineral water factory and above that, old St Cross Mill, that was the tobacco store.

The tide is in at Coppins Bridge, at its junction with the High Street. The crowd are stood roughly where Newport police station is today.

"The flood was on a Saturday morning. I heard the rain and I walked down Carisbrooke Road which was just about underwater to check my grandparents' house was all right. Then I walked down to the brewery and, of course, it was a real flood! Wrapped around the filler unit of the mineral water factory was a sofa from Kent's furniture store that had come down the river! We worked on, I can't remember how many days; people just turned up. We lost a lot of barrels of beer, some full, some empty, they were all washed out into the Solent. There was bottles everywhere, there was litter everywhere. You couldn't sell it because it had been contaminated.

Brickwoods did some brewing for us for a week or two but we were back up and running very quickly."

The crowd are eyeing the stores of Newport brewers, Mew Langton, situated at the bottom of Hunny Hill in what is now Halfords car park. St Cross Mill can just be seen on the right. The depth of floodwater in the store had reached nearly 20 feet when the pressure eventually blew out the side of the building and much of the contents, including a thousand tins of crisps, were swept away down the river. They would have made a perfect accompaniment to the many barrels of Mews beer which were swept away from the brewery at the same time. Over the next few weeks the barrels of beer were picked up by lucky finders as far away as the Solent.

by Brian Greening

The weather is a topic of conversation because it is a shared experience, and extremes give people plenty to talk about. My generation will always highlight the local floods of 1960, shown on the previous pages, and the great snow two years later. Two generations earlier, Islanders would tell of the tremendous snowfall of January 1881. Indeed, it was tradition, especially in the Ventnor district, that whenever a darts player threw a score of 81 there would be a chorus of "deep snow!" The "Wight-out" that year was preceded by a period of harsh frosts. The pond at Parkhurst Workhouse was frozen solid and hundreds of locals made good use of it as a skating rink. A small charge of one penny was made and Workhouse inmates were employed to continually sweep the surface. The scene was enhanced by the presence of the Workhouse Fife and Drum Band on the banks. The money raised went toward new band uniforms.

This was pre-*County Press* but the *IW Observer* and Hampshire newspapers covered the event and described how Ryde came to a virtual stop for several days. It was a time long before cars, but even the horse and carts were unable to negotiate the roads. Essentials such as coal, bread, vegetables and flour could not be supplied. The miller at Wootton, a Mr Souter, hitched seven horses to his carts but even the extra horse-power did not enable him to get right into Ryde, so men were employed to carry the sacks over a considerable distance. In Ryde High Street, the snow had piled each side of the road to a height of 16ft in some places. Once the main thoroughfares of the town had been cleared as far as Star Street, carts came up the High Street to load up with snow and take it down George Street to unload it on the shore.

The only good to come out of the weather event was that employment was found for many who would normally have been out of work at that time of the year. Among the worst to suffer were those in the St Helens district, where 'nature's white mantle' was to be found well above hedge height, while at Binstead it was 13 feet high. In the famous lovers' walk, between Ryde and Binstead, huge drifts were recorded, while on Bembridge Down, depths of up to 40ft were mentioned. Soup kitchens were set up in the town and coal was given to the poor. Ryde Gas Company distributed 1,000 bags of coke to the needy.

Above and top of page : Newport in the "Wight-out" of 1881

The Hampshire Advertiser reported the barracks at Parkhurst were not the best built or the most comfortable in normal times, so when in the January they were used for troops recently returned from India, the accommodation was less than popular. The troops marched from Cowes to the barracks through the deep snow but it became too much for two small drummer boys. They were so benumbed with cold they were taken in for a couple of days by a couple who worked at the barracks. At Parkhurst Prison the convicts were brought out to help clear the roads. When the thaw eventually came, the road from Newport to the barracks was, in places, ankle deep in water. In Newport at the end of January, it was reported the skies became black with threatening clouds and a further heavy fall of snow was expected. So dark were the skies, the Solent steamboats were kept in port.

The railway line between Sandown and Newport was temporarily impassable and it took the efforts of the soldiers at Sandown Barracks to clear it. Local labourers had refused to work for the 3/6d a day on offer and sought five shillings. The soldiers were pressed to do the task for the smaller day rate — and were rewarded by being pelted with snowballs. As always at these times, it was the aged poor who suffered most. Some went a week without bread or potatoes, to say nothing of the coldness of households that had run out of coal. In some places, it was said dog biscuits were considered a luxury. With coal unavailable in the villages, desperate people cut down apple and pear trees to burn. At Ventnor, while the snow was heavy, it was not as bad as the rest of the Island. However, one coal merchant removed the wheels from his trolley and converted it into a sleigh to deliver vast quantities of essential coal. Some of the older inhabitants said that it was similar to the weather when the Clarendon was wrecked at the back of the Island in 1836 and by coincidence, her ship's bell had been washed up and discovered by a waterman only two weeks before. The only other comparable previously recorded snowfall went back as far as 1799, when on one Sunday in February, a servant of Sir Richard Worsley was found frozen to death on Span Down. The following day, John Calbane, was found dead near Knowle Farm and Thomas Brown perished at St Lawrence. The day after that, a private in the IW Militia was found dead at Chale, he too having succumbed to exposure. The like of the snow of 1881 has probably never been equalled. We should remember houses in 1881 did not have the benefit of insulated lofts, double glazing, fitted carpets and central heating. Water pipes froze and subsequently bursts left householders without water for days. Until the 1950s we had to rely on coal fires — and it was nothing to go to bed and wake up with frost — on the inside of the windows!

The Mall under snow in 1881.

Compared to Newport in 1881, Ryde had a mild winter 29 years later. Did they call it global warming?
This photograph of Union Street in 1910 was taken by William Hogg, postcard producer, of Ryde.

by Alan Stroud

Until 1931 the Royal Pier Hotel stood at the bottom of Union Street in Ryde where today's roundabout now stands. Traffic coming down Union Street was faced with a notoriously difficult right-hand corner into what was then Pier Street, where the hotel stood on the left-hand side. One afternoon in March 1929, Charlie Wheeler, a driver for the Enterprise bus company, lost control of his bus as he drove down Union Street. In front of horrified lunchtime shoppers, two people were killed in the crash that followed as Charlie tried in vain to get round the sharp corner.

An Enterprise bus in the 1920s

On board were nine passengers and the conductor, Fred Bull, aged just 19. The bus, just in from East Cowes, had made its first stop at Cross Street where a lady and two little girls had the good luck to get off. Charlie then set off down Union Street with the remaining passengers, among them Jack Nunn, 45, a ship's rigger. returning to Essex after several days working at East Cowes.

Charlie told the subsequent inquest how he had driven down Union Street in third gear, "Everything went well until I reached the Post Office, when the bus shot ahead all at once. I tried the footbrake but there was nothing there and I pulled the handbrake as hard as I could and I shut off the engine." A witness at the inquest, Reg Yeldon, told the court, "I was outside the Post Office. My attention was first caught by the rolling of the body of the bus going from side to side, then I heard a loud noise which I think was the brakes being applied, or reversing the gears, and the bus then seemed to gather speed. It was travelling at about 30 miles an hour, the fastest I'd ever seen a bus go down the street."

Edward Stock, another witness, watched in horror as the bus hurtled past him, "The driver was going fast and I wondered if it was going to make the corner at the bottom at that pace."

The Royal Pier Hotel in 1907

Pier Street in 1913. On the right, the King Lud with its mock Tudor front and on the left, the side of the Royal Pier Hotel.

By now lunchtime shoppers were rooted to the spot, looking on in horror as the bus careered helplessly down the road. It was obvious to everyone watching that the bus and its occupants were in serious trouble. Winifred Teesdale told the court, "As it got near the bottom of Union Street I happened to look at the conductor who was on the bottom step. The bus got quicker and when it passed me it was over on its two nearside wheels."

Charlie took the corner at nearly 30 miles an hour, "I tried the best I could to swing round in to Pier Street. I got part of the way round but what happened then I don't know. I just trusted to Providence to get round."

Providence wasn't enough. Charlie had no chance and shocked onlookers saw the bus take the corner practically on two wheels and then topple over onto its left-hand side, felling a lamppost in the process. Jack Nunn was killed instantly, his body ending up lying on the ground in between the lamppost and the bus. He had suffered serious head injuries. Charlie was pulled from the wreckage through the broken windows, frightened and in a serious state of shock but somehow with only superficial injuries, "All I know is that I fell under the bus… But I was one of the lucky ones."

He was indeed. Poor Fred Bull was not so lucky. The 19 year old, one of a family of twelve, and described as "a promising young lad and a popular fellow," was found pinned face down on the road underneath the platform with much of the weight of the bus resting on him. Someone had telephoned for an ambulance and by the time it got there the crowd had lifted the platform and pulled him out.

He was taken to Ryde Hospital where he spoke briefly, complaining of chest pains, but quickly lapsed into unconsciousness, dying 15 minutes later. He had been a bus conductor for only twelve weeks.

Back at Pier Street, the wrecked bus lay on its side until mid-afternoon, "Her ripped front and her battered side with its broken glass presenting a sorry sight. A sense of gloom passed over the town." The Inquest jury exonerated Charlie Wheeler from all blame, describing the braking system of the bus as "useless." They also said something should be done about the dangerous corner. The Council, who had twice turned down the chance to buy the hotel, were now stung into action. They bought the hotel for £13,800 and it was demolished in October 1931 and Fred Bull, Jack Nunn and Pier Street passed quietly into history.

The Pier Hotel demolition in October 1931, recorded in a sketch by Tom Smitch of the *County Press.*

by Brian Greening

My memories of three Newport cinemas of yesteryear are very different to today's reality. Wonderful as the Coppins Bridge multiplex complex is, its forerunners were the Grand, the Odeon and the Medina. Even though the films had to be watched through a haze of cigarette smoke, we never spent more than one shilling (5p) to gain admittance to each cinema with all three having its own character and characters. How very different to today. Selecting Saturday's film depended on several factors. Firstly it had to have a 'U' certificate. An 'A' meant no admittance without adult company and believe it or not we would often ask a soldier from the barracks to

The Savoy Cinema, at the junction of Town Lane and Pyle Street, seen here following closure in December 1982, It started life in 1936 as the Odeon, changing its name to The Savoy in 1961,

accompany us in. One weekend, all the films in Newport were classified 'A' — and that meant taking a bus to East Cowes, to sit in their one and only flea pit, The Kings, to see John Mills in 'Hobson's Choice.' That odyssey added another 6d to the cost for a return bus ticket.

The Grand cinema in Mill Street was the least glamorous of the trio, simply because it had no upstairs seating. It was the easiest, however, into which to gain admission without paying. One of our group of short trouser-attired, snake-belt wearing lads, paid, took his seat and after five minutes visited the loo. He would then walk down the short passageway and open the emergency exit. At the back of the cinema was a double row of seats, in an alcove set aside for courting couples. Never old enough to sit in that promised land, I certainly recall one of my older brothers being a regular there. Just inside the cinema there was a large curtain sheltering those sitting in the front rows from the ever-opening door. Unfortunately, it was hung on a

The Savoy being demolished in 1984.

Jock Harper and niece outside the Grand

metal rail that perpetually begged a good application of WD40. The noise emitted each time the curtain parted was like a rusty nail scratching on corrugated tin.

Each cinema had a commissionaire and in Newport they were always of 'foreign' extraction. At the Grand was Jock Harper, an ex-Army man, always resplendent in his maroon uniform — but it must be said, often minus his false teeth. It was here I saw the film 'Rock Around the Clock', with Bill Haley.

One thing all three cinemas had in common was a crowd of queuing customers which, in the case of the Grand, often snaked up to the Castle Inn corner and around into the High Street. The Medina was in the High Street and not only showed films but put on Christmas pantomimes, as well as Sunday evening talent contests. Judging was by audience applause and sadly this was not always the fairest way. At the time, Michael Holliday was a famous crooner and he made a record entitled 'The Story of My Life.' One aspiring imitator got on stage and tried to sing it but he stopped every two lines to fumble in his pocket for a piece of paper bearing the words. He was so bad he was brilliant, and he brought the house down but common sense prevailed and somehow he came second that evening to a one-legged Irish busker playing comb and paper. Our love of the silver screen knew no bounds and when the film 'David and Bathsheba' came to town in 1951, starring Gregory Peck and Susan Hayward; we little boys went crazy, as the heroine was seen to take a bath in asses milk, with a large cleavage clearly visible. One advantage the Medina had was that it was directly opposite Jolliffe's shop so after watching the film you could simply cross the road and indulge in one of their legendary peppery meat pies and a bottle of brown ale.

The cinema par excellence had to be the Odeon. A clock inside had letters instead of numerals on its face that spelled out 'ODEON' with a space where numbers three and nine should have been. It is only recently I discovered the letters stood for "Oscar Deutsche Entertains Our Nation," after the man who opened up Odeon cinemas all over the country. By the time Oscar died in 1941, there were 258 Odeons throughout the land. It cost six or nine pence to go downstairs or one shilling to go upstairs which had the advantage of being able to exit the fire escape at the end of the evening without standing for the National Anthem. That gave an important extra ten minutes with the young lady you had spent all that money on, under the railway arches on Coppin's Bridge before putting her on a bus home.

At the Odeon, the commissionaire was Taffy Reece, another ex-military man who came to the fore on Saturday morning matinees. There was always a weekly serial that ended each week with the hero in a precarious predicament, strapped possibly to a table, whilst a circular saw advanced upon him. Usually too, there was a cowboy film, in which Roy Rogers, his horse, Trigger, and sidekick, Gabby Hayes, starred. Other cowboys were Hopalong Cassidy and Lash La Rue, the latter being an expert with his bullwhip in bringing down the baddies.

Sometimes we would get a comedy film starring the Bowery Boys or the Marx brothers. It was advisable to go upstairs on those mornings, as those seated in the lower section got pelted with empty ice cream cartons during the interval, a time when Taffy earned his money.

Sadly, all three cinemas have gone the way of many other landmark buildings, like the cattle market in South Street and Newport football pitch. Our railway station at Station Approach, is now, ironically, buried beneath the site of an undertaker's establishment and the railway viaduct at Coppin's Bridge is now the site of an horrendous roundabout.

The Odeon staff in 1937.

by Alan Stroud

In the sixties, as television went from black-and-white into colour, so did Britain itself. There was an explosion in fashion, the arts and especially music. Pop music had always been important to Britain's teenagers but in the sixties it became almost compulsory. Three Islanders played their own special part in the Sixties music revolution.

In 1968, three Totland brothers, Ray, Ronnie and Bill Foulk put on a one-day festival at Godshill. It was a success, attracting 10,000 fans and led them to put on the 1969 Wootton Festival with headline act Bob Dylan. Ray told Isle of Wight Radio's Tom Stroud in 2010, "We didn't have to talk to the local authorities. We didn't need a licence. We just got on with it. We had no interference at all and to get Dylan to appear was an international coup. He was like the Messiah to a lot of people, a huge name. When we got a telegram to say he and the Band would accept, well, you could have knocked me down with a feather. I had to go and meet him in New York the next week. I was 23, I hadn't been abroad before, I had no passport, nothing."

Dylan was signed and a few weeks later, the festival was upon them. "It was an excellent site at Wootton. I remember arriving there on the Friday night. I drove through the lanes with lots of people everywhere, went backstage and I walked up on the stage and got a glimpse of the 200,000 audience. That was the first time I'd seen the arena full of people and it took my breath away. That was an incredible feeling. Suddenly I felt, 'We've done it. We've pulled it off. We've got this huge audience and they're all here.' It was full, a massive sea of people and there was a group performing and everybody was enjoying themselves. That really was a quite wonderful moment." The festival went on to be a huge success but not everyone loved it, "An excuse for dirty people to behave in a dirty manner," wrote one *County Press* reader.

A crowd of 150,000 at the 1969 festival. In his book, *"Stealing Dylan from Woodstock,"* Ray Foulk gives a 'behind the scenes' account of the trials and tribulations of attracting Bob Dylan to a field in Wootton.

In the early 60s British pop music could be heard all over the world – except in Britain where pop was confined to two hours a week on the BBC Light Programme. To fill the vacuum, in 1964 'pirate radio' arrived to break the BBC monopoly. For the rest of the 60s, British teenagers could listen to all-day pop music transmitted from radio stations broadcasting quite legally from ships anchored just outside territorial waters, where they were beyond the reach of British law. A little known fact is that four of these ships were rigged by the Cowes company Spencer

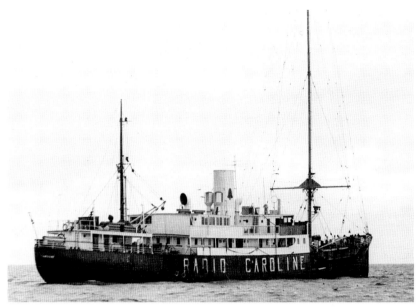

The Radio Caroline North ship, the Fredericia, rigged by Harry Spencer

Rigging, run by Harry Spencer. In a 1996 interview he told IW Radio's John Hannam, "An Irishman, Ronan O'Rahilly, wanted to start a radio station. I kept getting phone calls from his partner, a man called Alan Crawford, who said, 'We want you to come and talk about masts and rigging. You know about masts and rigging,' and I said, 'Well, I hope I do, a little!' So off I went to his office, the Merit music company in Soho and I thought, 'What an odd place to have a shipping office.' I didn't know it was going to be a pirate radio ship at that time. It was described to me as a weather ship. So I went in and I was asked, 'What height of mast do you think you could put in this ship?' and I said, 'I suppose about 190 feet, something like that.' I met the captain, who then told me the mast was for a radio antenna and eventually I persuaded him that you could stand a mast up this size by telling him that his grandparents must have sailed around in vessels this size with a lot of canvas on, not just a radio antenna, and with that he had me over in Amsterdam within the next two hours, with no passport. That was the start. I then got the job to mast and rig two radio ships, Radio Caroline North which was anchored off the Isle of Man and Radio Caroline South which was in the Thames estuary where we met Simon Dee and Tony Blackburn, who was a boy of 16, an enthusiastic youngster who wanted to play the turntables. Eventually we went on to do Radio Scotland and then Radio 270 off Scarborough."

The pirates were a huge success for the next three years, attracting millions of listeners and hundreds of advertisers. Everybody loved the pirates - Except the Labour government. In August 1967, the Marine Offences Act was passed, making it illegal for British subjects to assist or work for offshore stations in any shape or form, and one by one the pirates closed down apart from Radio Caroline, who continued broadcasting for another six months before they too, closed down. To replace the pirates, Radio One was launched but it was a poor substitute for the 24 hours a day of pop that the pirates had provided, and in response amateur pirate stations sprang up across the country. One of them was the Island's very own 'Radio Sound City' broadcasting from their studios at Porchfield – or to be more precise, the bedroom of 18-year-old Richard Brimson, then an apprentice at Plessey, Cowes. Using a powerful medium wave transmitter built by Richard, the station attracted a lot of listeners during its short life and even boasted its own car stickers, but when it became the subject of a photo-feature in the *Portsmouth Evening Echo* the authorities decided to act. One Saturday afternoon, shortly after the article appeared, Post Office officials descended on Porchfield and raided the station, actually forcing it to close down in mid-broadcast. Speaking today, Richard says, "I went into pirate radio with my eyes open. I knew I'd get caught eventually and I'd already put aside £30 which was the

The well equipped studios of Radio Sound City with DJ Kevin Lee at the microphone. Inset : A Radio Sound City car sticker.

average fine for operating a pirate station, so I was shocked to be fined £150 with £15 costs. It took me a year to pay it back at £3 a week - I was only earning £10 a week at that time."

Money well spent, some might say, to stand alongside Ray Foulk and Harry Spencer – all three of them enterprising Islanders who each in their own way made a mark on the Sixties.

by Brian Greening

I was recently in a pub when two groups met up who obviously had not seen each other for several years. Within less than five minutes photographs had been taken, sent across to relatives in America and two old friends were to be seen not only talking to each other but actually seeing each other. Modern technology passes me by and I confess I found it remarkable.

Just over one hundred years ago the year 1915 was very different. The country was only just embarking on the long journey of the First World War. It was one of death and glory, both at home and overseas, and it was

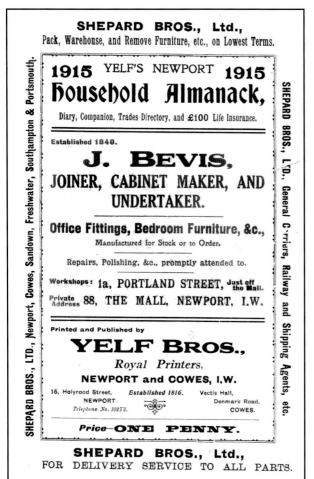
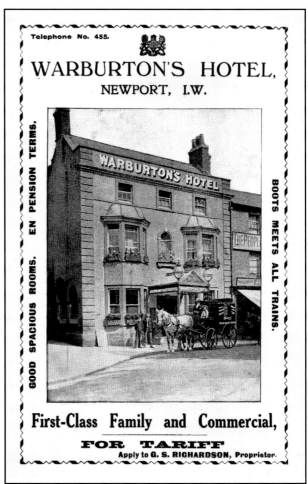

Above, and opposite, the front cover and pages from Yelf's 1915 Household Almanack.

faithfully recorded in a local review of the year booklet, called Yelf's Almanac. In those days, people were compelled to wait for their news, as was Mrs. Urry, who lived in Orchard Street. It would have been a good couple of weeks before she would learn that all three of her sons were missing, presumed dead, fighting abroad for their country. The Almanack did tell of eight young Newport men who joined up in the first recruitment rally in the town who were lost with the sinking of the Royal Edward transport ship in the Aegean Sea on August 13th. Their names were given as Privates Charles Young, Cecil Bull, William Hunnybun, Charles Pierce, T. Matthews, Harold Gallop, Reginald Hollis and Charles Wolfe.

At home, Newport's resigning mayor was Mr. A. E. Harvey, who many will recall as the owner of that wonderful cake shop with a restaurant and tea rooms above in Newport High Street. He had bravely carried out his duties for two years and not surprisingly found that period particularly stressful. Much of his time had been spent raising money for the war effort, and the IW Territorial Active Service Benefit Fund had been enriched by more than £2,000 in the first year. Other good causes included the sending of 300 blankets to the military at Parkhurst Barracks and more than 5,000 garments, mattresses and pillow cases, principally to the Belgians, who were among the first to be crushed by the Germans. Much of the account of the happenings of 1915 touched on the terrible losses inflicted on the IW Rifles at Gallipoli. It is worth noting, however, that as these troops did not withdraw until mid-December of that year, the writer was not aware of just how terrible their losses would turn out to be.

Turning away from those terrible reports coming back from the front, the Island suffered another loss that year with the death of Sir Charles Seely. His family will be remembered for their generosity in providing Newport with its water supply that was drawn from the Gatcombe Estate, and the provision of many cottages in Gatcombe and Chillerton for farm workers. They also helped fund a library that took the family name at Nodehill. Indeed it was much earlier in 1889 that Sir Charles gave £50 toward forming a library in Carisbrooke, insisting that it include the novels of Sir Walter Scott, including Rob Roy, Ivanhoe, Captain Marryatt's Children of the New Forest, and novels by Dickens. Another to pass away that year included local character Mr. Alexander Grey, better known as Holy Joe, who died in the old Globe public house on Coppin's Bridge. He was an itinerant preacher, touring villages preaching the word of God and seeking a meal for his efforts. It was said it would bring good luck to any baby if it was kissed by him.

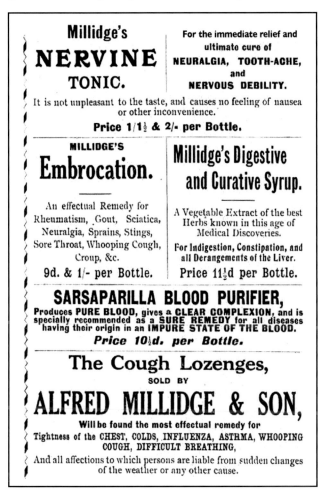
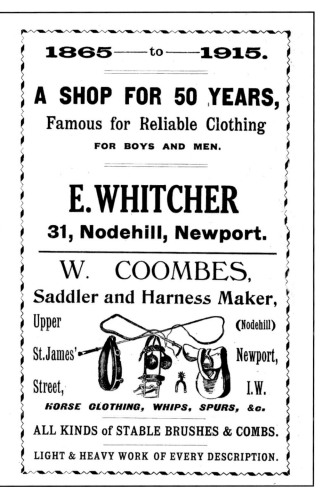
Another who died that year was Mr John Samuel White who, at the age of just twenty had in 1858, started in business for himself at East Cowes. By 1885, he had built the first 150ft-long torpedo craft and this led to a 200 feet long vessel being built. As a result, further orders for torpedo gunboats were received and the rest is local history for his name will always be associated with Cowes and East Cowes for the jobs that were created and the wide range of ships that were built.

There were advertisements for businesses that eventually traded in the town for more than a century, unlike the majority of today's traders who seem to disappear after two years. Yelf Bros itself was a printer in Holyrood Street as early as 1816 whilst Whitchers the 'Wight Man's clothier', Coombes, the harness and saddle maker and Jordan and Stanley, grocers, all had premises in Nodehill. They were joined by J. E. Snellgrove, painter and decorators. Walter Rugg had, in my youth, at least five shops in Newport selling snuff, cigarettes, tobacco and Havana cigars, the latter selling in 1915 for twenty-five shillings per hundred.

You could not fail to observe the number of postal collections that were made each day from the pillar and wall boxes scattered around the town. Those at the Town Hall, the Corn Exchange, St Thomas's Square, Nodehill and Trafalgar Road were emptied seven times a day between 6.15am and 7.15pm, the last collection being at 8.30pm from the Town Hall pillar box. If you lived 'out in the sticks,' such as Fairlee Road, Avondale Road, Clarence Road or Cedar Hill, your collections would vary in number from between three and five. There were three deliveries of mail each day from London but, sadly, just one on Sundays. Today you risk hypothermia as you queue by the refrigerators in Newport's only in town Post Office that is set up in a supermarket. Yelf's Almanac for that year certainly illustrated times when access to news and information was very different to that of today, and I am told we have to put this down to progress.

THREE MEN IN A BOAT - AND THEN THERE WERE TWO. BUT WAS IT MURDER?

by Alan Stroud

It was just after ten on a dark Monday night in September 1905, "altogether a nasty night," said the *Isle of Wight Chronicle*. Three sailors belonging to the yacht Iolanthe put off in a rowing boat from Watchhouse slipway at Cowes (seen below) to return to their yacht but when they arrived, only two sailors were in the boat. "A sensational case" said the *County Press* when one of them was charged with "feloniously killing and slaying" the missing man. And it was about to get more sensational.

Initially, four men got in the boat, but one, William Barton, a steward on the Iolanthe, got out before it left. His evidence in the subsequent murder trial was to raise some eyebrows. In the boat when it pulled away was John Kitchen, 'a small man of very quiet and inoffensive character'; William Hockings, 'a man of considerable size and strength', and Albert Dallimore. When Hockings and Dallimore arrived alone at the Iolanthe a few minutes later they told the captain that Kitchen had jumped over the side and they had seen him pull himself out of the water at the slipway. In fact, Kitchen's body was found floating in shallow water near the Esplanade on Thursday morning. The next day an inquest was held and heard how the men had come ashore, visited some Cowes pubs and that just after ten a group of locals had watched as they set off for the yacht from the slipway.

The witnesses all agreed that the men appeared to be sober and that on the slipway Hockings had an angry argument with a man named Cotton. One said, 'When the boat put off, Hockings said to Kitchen, "That was your — chum, and I will serve you the same if you say two words." Kitchen said, "I've done nothing." Then Hockings threw the oars down and went for Kitchen and knocked him about a great deal, striking him very heavily. Kitchen was a small man and was in the bottom of the boat while this was going on. Kitchen did not try to hit him back. Dallimore did nothing to interfere.' Henry Caws of Cowes said, "I saw Hockings punching Kitchen unmercifully. I told him it was a cowardly bit of work. Kitchen took out his handkerchief and wiped the blood from his face as the boat put off."

The inquest found that "deceased received his injuries from Hockings, and died by drowning, but there is no evidence to show how he came into the water." As the inquest ended, Hockings was charged with Kitchen's murder but outside, "he was cheered by a large crowd and shook hands with several of his friends."

The one man who knew what happened that night was the third man in the boat, Albert Dallimore but he did not attend the inquest because he was dreading it — Something, or someone, was worrying him. So much so, that the night before the inquest, he went to his cabin and hanged himself.

At the inquest into his death, Captain Love of the Iolanthe was asked : 'Did you have conversations about what took place in the boat? : Yes, a good many. I asked him and Hockings what they had done with Kitchen and they said he jumped over the side and got out on the causeway. Dallimore seemed low and depressed when I talked

Cowes High Street in the 1890s.

to him. Dallimore asked how he thought he would get on. I said "tell the truth whatever you do. That will carry you through. Don't keep anything back to try and save other people." I was not exactly surprised to hear he had committed suicide. Dallimore was a man who would take anything to heart"

When Barton gave evidence at the trial he was no keener on giving evidence than Dallimore had been. Unbelievably, he told the court he "could not say in which part of the boat Kitchen was." Q. You say you do not know? - No, I don't. Q. Did you see any blow struck? - No. I did not. I saw another boat and I was trying to keep my eye on it. - Q. You could see another boat, but you could not see what was going on in your own boat? - Yes. Q. That is all the account you can give of what took place that evening? - Yes. The Chairman : Do you understand the oath you have taken to speak the truth, the whole truth, and nothing but the truth? - Yes, sir. Q. Then take care you do. It seems to me you need a caution very badly. Is that all the information you are going to give the Court? - I cannot give you any more. Q. I must caution you that you are liable to be tried for perjury if you don't tell the truth. - That is the truth."

Hockings testimony was not much better. He insisted nothing had gone on in the boat between him and Kitchen, who he referred to as "poor Jack." The judge addressed the jury, pointing out that all the witnesses were agreed, and the only evidence that disagreed with them was that of Hockings. The jury retired for 20 minutes and announced that they had found the prisoner not guilty. "There was some attempt at applause in Court, which was immediately suppressed." And with that, Hockings left the Court a free man and - some would say - a very lucky man.

Cowes Parade and the slipway where a boat cast off into the night and three men became two.

A HIGH PRESSURE JOURNEY

by Brian Greening

Moving heavy loads is not anything new, if we consider the work that was entailed all those years ago by those building the Pyramids and Stonehenge. What those intrepid workers, however, never had to do was to negotiate moving along our wonderful Island's roads, that although far from perfect today were much less so over one hundred years ago. Upon being formed in 1890 one of the first tasks undertaken by our new Isle of Wight County Council was to find a site and build an Asylum, as up until then all Island patients needing such a facility had to be transported across to Fareham, the cost being a heavy drain on the Island's financial resources. After considering several sites at Redway, Furzey Hurst, Marvel, Longdown and Hale, the site at Whitecroft was finally chosen, the cost of the land being £4150. To build the Asylum cost an additional £4150, that was offset by the fact six million bricks were made on the site using the excavated clay and sand.

Much use would have been made of the railway link to Blackwater for delivering some materials but transporting a heavy 30ft-long, 16-ton boiler up Sandy Lane was not feasible. This large load had already been transported by boat from Southampton to Newport Quay, and unloaded opposite where today's Quay Arts Centre is. That, however, was when the real work began. Had health and safety existed then, the boiler would not have left the Quay. There were no toe-protector boots, hard hats or fluorescent jackets to wear but a job was there to be done using local muscle and ingenuity.

As there was no crane large enough, the boiler had to be rolled off the boat on to a low trailer that Shepard Bros used for transporting Portland stone to Isle of Wight monumental masons. The eventual journey to Whitecroft would take eight hours and would have to overcome several obstacles, the first within a matter of yards of moving off.

Taking a rest at the Simeon Monument, Carisbrooke Mall, en route to Whitecroft.

The Quay Street turning into the High Street wrenched off the rear wheels of the trailer and it took three hours to forge a repair. It was then onward, up the High Street and Carisbrooke Mall where a rest was taken by the Simeon Monument. Then the load progressed up Castle Road, before having to negotiate the steep incline past the cemetery, a task that was achieved quite successfully by the vast team of over twenty horses harnessed three abreast. Going downhill was, however, to prove more difficult and on negotiating the descent at Little Whitcombe corner, a winch was used to hold the heavy load back — but this decided to malfunction. At such times it is preferable to have one man in charge giving orders but on this occasion there were continual differences of opinion between Frank Shepard and local wheelwright Frederick Guy. Their colourful language was recalled

The boiler which had been brought from the mainland on Croucher Bros' boat the Whip. From here, however, responsibility became that of Shepard Bros.

years later by the then thirteen-year-old Arthur Williams, who had taken the day off school. Arthur would, in the ensuing years, fight for his country in both France and Jerusalem and return a much changed man. He would, in time too, become a local celebrity and adopt for himself the title of the Mayor of Gatcombe, wearing as his regalia an old lavatory chain on which was mounted the pendulum of a clock. Let me quickly add here that Arthur was not an imbecile but simply one of what today is a dying breed — a real character. It is to Arthur that much of this story is to be credited. He recalled in booklets, left with his daughter, that at one point the load had to be moved just twenty-feet before a winch could take over and he remembered this being done by just two horses, Traveller and Lad, that belonged to Mr Urry at Hill Farm, Gatcombe. Arthur recalled these two magnificent beasts with taut muscles being almost on their knees before moving the load that short distance. Hawsers wrapped around nearby trees also acted as a means of holding the load back on the journey, as well as every available man holding on to ropes. The health and safety man at that time would probably by now either have called into a local public house and downed several neat whiskies, or popped in the nearby Nunnery to say a fervent prayer.

Our Island ancestors were, however, a doughty lot and the heavy load eventually arrived safely at Whitecroft, where it stayed in the road overnight, the transporters confident that no local vandals would steal it. In total, there were just as many men as there were horses used in completing this task, but if Arthur was to be believed, the expletives he learned far outnumbered the number of men and horses added together. That road to the asylum has changed little in more than one hundred years but should a similar task be performed today, it would make the journey in around fifteen minutes. Not, before I might add, the council would have closed the road, advised of diversions and erected several sets of traffic lights.

By the time another boiler was needed for the Workhouse at St Mary's, Shepard Bros had acquired two more steam-powered road traction engines and there were others available. Even then, three of these engines plus a threshing machine, which was harnessed to the boiler load itself, had to be used to negotiate Hunnyhill. This is where the practicality of the operation was lost to me but apparently an unexpected problem arose because all that load caused the heavy engine to rear upwards, taking weight off the front wheels and making steering impossible. By placing the chain connected from engine number two around the base of the smoke stack of engine number three, the pulling power was maintained and the downward pull allowed the third engine to be successfully manoeuvred.

Had they undertaken this job before 1828, their task would have been even more difficult. That was the year that Hunnyhill was lowered and the bridge at the bottom widened to provide an easier access into Newport.

A painting of the scene as the boiler passed the Nunnery in Whitcombe Road.

by Alan Stroud

In the early 1980s Colin Fairweather and I recorded nine Islanders talking about their childhood and working lives for our book 'Island Voices.' We were lucky. One of them was the splendid Reg Davies of Newport, then in his seventies. In 1923, 14 year old Reg became a bus conductor with Leonard Dodson's Vectis Bus Company, better known today as Southern Vectis. It was a perfect match and Reg went on to enjoy a lifelong love affair with his buses, taking literally thousands of photographs of them. Here are just three of the many stories Reg told us, all from the 1930's. The first involves conductors who picked up used tickets from the floor to resell them and pocket the money...

"We were always getting fired by Dodson - 'you're fired" he would say. Only he didn't used to say that. He used to use a little bit of French with it as well. He used to point his pipe at you, "You're —— sacked!"

"We went in Yelf's in the Square and had a cup of tea; I've got a photograph with old Gerald outside with me in the doorway."

One day I had Charlie Taylor on with me, doing Ryde to Newport, and there was a woman to get out where Fairlee garage is now. It had been raining and we had these huge balloon tyres on the back. I gave Charlie a bell to stop and being a big powerful chap he whacked on his brake, whoof!, and we skidded and away we went across the road and pitched on a wall. The wheels were hanging over the side in the drop into the garden and Char, I'll always remember, said, 'There you are, madam. Out the back way instead of the front!' There was a picture taken of us stood by the bus. 'Course, when we got into Newport, Dodson got his pipe out like a revolver and he says, 'You're fired!' So Charlie says, 'Come on then! Give us my cards.' 'Course it was all bluff. Dodson says, 'Go away! Come back and get your cards later.' Well, we didn't have a bus to drive so we went in Yelf's in the Square and had a cup of tea; I've got a photograph with old Gerald outside with me in the doorway. George Hyde came in after a while and he gave us our orders for the next day. 'You can shove off,' he says, 'There isn't any buses for you.' Charlie said 'Well that's one way of getting an evening off,' and Dodson was stood behind the wall there and he heard. He says, 'You're fired!' he says, 'You're fired...'"

"I was off duty one day and I took a bus to Sandown and Dave Peach was conductor on it. When we got to Yarbridge crossroads, who should jump on but Titchy Dean, the inspector. Well, David, he collapsed on the seat in front! Just collapsed! Me and Titchy undid his collar and laid him down and when we pulled in at Sandown I had David in my arms, patting his hands, and Titchy was quite concerned. He said, 'We'll have to get him a doctor.' The passengers were getting off the bus and I was looking at David. I didn't know what the devil was the matter with him; I thought he was going to die - but as I cradled him he winked at me! I was flabbergasted! I was just going to tell Titchy but I held back and Dave came round and moaned, 'Oooh.' Titchy said, 'Well, he won't be all right to Newport.' I said, 'I'm going back there, I'll take over if anything happens,' so Titchy got off. 'Course, directly he jumped off, David sprang to life, 'Cooh, that was a close squeeze! I had about six dud tickets on my rack.' He'd sold five or six of these bloomin' duds to the people on the bus! If he hadn't fainted old Titchy would have gone round and he'd have been caught. He would have been sacked!...

"There was a woman, Miss Hague, who was 'pretty friendly' with Leonard and she had a free pass. Frank Salero was driving this particular day and Miss Hague wanted to get off in Lower St James Street and 'course,

"Char, I'll always remember, said, 'There you are, madam. Out the back way instead of the front!'"

Reg leaving the Island in 1994, aged 87, with little more than hand luggage, to live in Australia with his daughter Ros. Reg died there in 2001.

Frank pulled up and he put a bit of a jerk on and she tripped over the gear lever in the centre gangway and she went down – whoomp - straight into this hole where the door was, and 'course Frank started, 'Haw, haw, haw.' Laughed, you see. So 'course, she reported him to Dodson. We both had to go and see him. Dodson says, 'When Miss Hague got out of the bus, you threw her over. And not only did you do that but you laughed at her.' Frank said, 'So'd you, Governor, if you'd seen her bloomers!' Dodson says, 'You're fired. You're fired!'

"One day an insurance agent got on the bus with his wife, regular customers they were, and I got up to take their fares and this chap said to me,"Look, my wife got some oil on her dress. Brand new dress," And she had this stain of oil. He said, "Good mind to claim," you know, joking. And I said, "Oh, go and claim from the old man," I said, "He's got plenty of money." And about two days afterwards, Dodson called me upstairs. I went in and who should be sitting there but this chap and his wife. "Hello, Reg," they said, and Dodson says, "Is this the conductor that was on the bus?" They said, "Yes." So he said, "Got some grease on the ..." "Yes" I said, "it was on her dress," I said. Pleased as punch I was! And he said, "Oh, that's all right then." So the couple went off and of course I went to go out behind them. when he shouts "Just a minute!!" he says. Called me back. He said, "Oh, so you go and see Mr Dodson!" he says. "He'll pay you out in compensation!" He'd paid this woman out ten pounds for a bloomin' dress that cost about thirty bob... He said, "You're fired!" Only he didn't used to say that. He used to use a bit of French with it, you know, always the language with it. He used to point the pipe at you... "You're ——— sacked!"

A 'Monstrous Absurdity' that lasted For 100 Years

by Brian Greening

As someone who can recall the days when we had an Island-wide rail network, I got to wondering just how much readers know of the struggles that took place before the railways finally came to the Island in the first place? From as early as 1840 it took over twenty years of opposition by the local landowners before the first train ran from Cowes to Newport in 1862. At that time, it was reported that passengers who made that first return journey were amazed to find that when they arrived back home the breakfast items were still on the table.

In the beginning, these large landowners were vehemently against the scheme and an article in Punch magazine said if the railways ever arrived, the Island would look like a hot cross bun, with railway lines criss-crossing it. Among these landowners was Lord Yarborough of Appuldurcombe, but it was his son, the Hon. Dudley Pelham, who became the mouthpiece for the group opposed to the railway's introduction. In a letter to the press he described it as a "monstrous absurdity" and said railroad schemes were a gambling bubble that would burst with a just a few people making money. The majority would long regret their speculations, he said. He then listed his objections. 1. The railways would depreciate the value of property in towns and in the country; 2. They would be injurious to agricultural interests, toll-gate revenue would be lost and there were no commercial interests that would benefit, and none would be created. He further added that tourists would prefer the current mode of transport and would not wish to be whisked across the countryside "at speed." Landed property on the Island

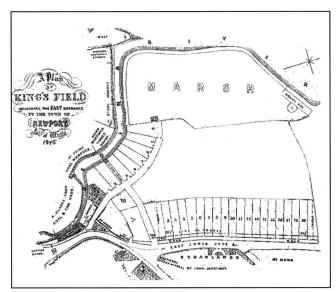

A map of Kingsfield Terrace building plots in 1845 when the undeveloped town quay was marshland.

was of a high value compared to the mainland and, although a railway might increase the number of tourists, they would have the effect of keeping away many people of rank or competence, the money spending class, (his words, not mine). He then asked why the Island had been selected as a royal residence, why was it such a popular and fashionable place and why property here was so valuable? His reasoning was simple. It was because, as yet, it had not been invaded by the railways.

In time, these leading landowners called public meetings on the issue and, sadly, the working class of the Island who attended, followed them like sheep; not surprising really as they would be seen to oppose the views of their employers and their jobs might be at risk. As an alternative there was a second scheme suggested, that of dredging the River Medina, to enable larger ships to enter Newport Harbour. However, there were voices who spoke out against the river dredging scheme and one gentleman who wrote to the newspapers put forward his reasons for supporting a railway. It was intended the railway should link Cowes, Newport and Ventnor and the villages en-route. He described Cowes as a seaport of immense value and importance. It was, he said, the "Liverpool of the Island." It had, he claimed, streets of vast breadth and two chapels. (Here he was clearly confusing West Cowes with its developing cousin at East Cowes.) He went on to say there were improvements being made to the town's buildings, and its harbour and its waterways were a forest of masts. At any one time one might see as many as a dozen American sea captains in town. Newport contained just over four thousand residents and was a town where business and fashion, commerce and elegance combined. The church of St. Thomas, admittedly, he said, was tumbling down from neglect, and a truer statement was never made, as in 1854 it had to be rebuilt.

Ventnor, he went on, was a place of nearly one thousand souls, where fashion, good health and salubriousness abounded. It was an attraction for invalids, most of whom already had respirators, the only contrivance for protecting the lungs of second-class travellers. The railways offered the only practicable means of locomotion. The traffic between Cowes, Newport and Ventnor was at all times quite stunning, especially in the winter, with coaches, wagons and vehicles of every kind, making the lives of the toll-gate operators extremely busy. The biggest argument in favour of the railways, he said, was the Island was basically flat and ideal for rail, avoiding the need for deep cuttings and fearful tunnels.

Time marched on and a great deal of money was spent promoting the river scheme. Slowly, however, the railway scheme gained favour and the landowners ceased their objections when they realized how much compensation they would get for allowing a rail line through their estates. Mr. Pring, a Newport councillor and a strong advocate for the railways, stated that there was less stress and fatigue in travelling by train, as he had found when going from Liverpool to Manchester, than going by a horse-drawn coach from Newport to Ventnor, where in winter, its streets were entirely impassable because of mud.

There you have the arguments put forward all those years ago. In hindsight, we could be critical of aspects of them all. However, common sense did prevail and for almost one hundred years we enjoyed that special smell, the hissing of steam and the comfort of travelling the Island without encountering one pot-hole or, indeed, a single set of traffic lights, and we were able to smile and raise two fingers at the impatient car drivers as they were held up by closed gates at level crossings at such places as Shide, Blackwater, and Horringford. Imagine how they would react today, road rage would take off.

A coal train in the Medina Wharf sidings on the Cowes to Newport line.

THE END OF THE END OF THE PIER SHOW

by Alan Stroud

Ryde has a problem with the sea. It's too far away. To be precise, at low tide it's nearly half a mile away. At the same time its proximity to Portsmouth makes it the shortest Solent crossing so in times gone by the inconvenient half mile slog across the sands was seen as a price worth paying. Not that there weren't complaints. "Ryde is divided into Upper and Lower" wrote one traveller in 1808. "The lower, or old village, is built along the shore and is chiefly inhabited by seafaring persons. At low water, landing from the boats is performed in small carts, drawn by a single horse. Thus, seated on each side of this machine, driven by a man who sits in front, a ludicrous journey is performed before we reach the town." A pier was the answer. It was begun in 1813, opening the following year. It was an immediate success and by the 1850s had established itself as one of Ryde's main attractions.

Today the pier is just a means of getting from A to B but in a previous life it was also a place of entertainment. In 1895 a 500 seat concert hall, the Pavilion Ballroom, was opened at the end of the pier alongside shops, sun decks and refreshment rooms. It was an immediate success, transforming the pier into a mecca for visitors and tourists who came to take the air and by the turn of the last century the pier had become *the* place to be seen promenading.

Promenaders taking the air on Ryde Pier in 1907, the Pavilion Ballroom in the background.

With three million customers a year for ferries and steamer excursions the pier prospered and by 1939 boasted a 'casino', and even a pub, 'The First and Last.' but the war and changing fashions saw the pier's fortunes reverse almost overnight. By the late 1940s, its glory days were all but over when Clive Norman, father of Philip Norman the noted author, became its new owner in 1949 and took on the challenge of breathing new life into it. In his 2003 autobiography 'Babycham Night,' Philip Norman describes his childhood spent growing up at the end of the pier. It is a beautifully observed account of the simpler way of life that was the 1950s with the added attraction that many of the places and names in the book will be familiar to Island readers.

The first task for Clive Norman was to rename the ballroom. Philip Norman wrote, "My father seemed on a creative high that nothing could check. His master stroke, I thought, was in choosing the new name. He told me how he had found the answer in the screaming white flocks that haunted the sky and sea out there. What else could he call his new creation but the Seagull?" What else, indeed?

For the next twenty years the Seagull was home to the sound of teacups and electric organ - and on occasion, the odd splash. "One Sunday my father asked our help in throwing a grand piano into the sea. It had stood on the Pavilion's stage for years, dust-sheeted and forgotten; now, to make space for the electronic organ that was to play in his new Seagull Ballroom, he'd decided to get rid of it in the way we disposed of most unwanted items.

Posters on the side of the Seagull Ballroom. The Pink Floyd cancelled, the Small Faces stepping in. From Roger George Clark's 2008 book "*Perfect England - The Isle of Wight in the 1960s.*"

An aerial shot of the pier head in the mid-1980s. The skeleton of metal piles that once supported the Seagull Ballroom can be seen in the sea at the top of the picture.

A gang of volunteers carried the piano out of the Pavilion and heaved it over the rail. Amazingly, it floated and for hours afterwards could be seen bobbing slowly out on the tide towards the shipping lanes. I'd like to be on the Queen Mary when she comes in this evening,' my father said, grinning. 'Someone is going to look out of a porthole and not be able to believe their eyes'."

By the 1960s, holidays abroad were affecting ferry passenger numbers and the pier went into decline. In the mid-1960s, local club owner, Clive Meddick, took over the Seagull and it became a popular music venue and the Saturday night home of acts like The Nice, Dave Dee, Dozy, etc, and The Small Faces. In the heady 'summer of love' of 1967, the ballroom was briefly re-named the 'Big L Speakeasy' when it became associated with one of the most successful pirate radio stations, Radio London, or 'Big L'. It was a short lived alliance. Within two weeks of the photo being taken, most of the pirates, including Radio London, had closed down following legislation by the Labour government. As the sixties came to an end so did the ballroom - due to structural problems. The last musical act act to tread the boards of the Seagull ballroom was Traffic in September 1968.

The Seagull Ballroom complete with tasteful Southern Vectis booth in 1960.

Two years later the Seagull was no more. The fabric of the building had deteriorated and Ryde's pleasure dome was demolished. Today a gaping hole and rusty stilts peering above the waves are all that remain. The Victorian trippers are no more, the afternoon teas have been cleared away and Dave Dee, alas, can no longer bend it. Wightlink operate the pier today and where past generations once took the air there is now a car park.

It's all too beautiful.

Extracts from "Babycham Night," published 2003 by Macmillan, appear by kind permission of Philip Norman.

by Brian Greening

What street in Newport has been home over the years to at least five public houses, a Poor House, a prison, a police station, and a printer that traded for more than one hundred and fifty years? Answer: Holyrood Street, where the pubs included the Vine, the Albany Tavern, the Royal Oak, (now part of Hurst's) the Medina Inn, and the Sun Inn that dated back to around 1750, when it was the venue for glamorous balls attended by the great and the good of the Island. It was in 1774 that two of the Island's foremost members of the aristocracy bought an old building at the bottom of Holyrood Street. The two were Leonard Holmes, who lived at Westover and whose family had inherited the right to nominate Newport and Yarmouth's MPs, and Thomas Blachford, whose family were long connected with Osborne House. The property they acquired for £180 was Newport's obsolete Poor House, which the authorities decided would be ideal as a local prison or, as it was then known, the Bridewell. For the next seventy five years it became a place best avoided. Not only were offenders imprisoned there, men and boys were whipped inside those walls and there was a punishment known as the treadmill where they walked miles but got nowhere, just like the donkey in the wheel at Carisbrooke. There was also the crank, where inmates were forced to complete a set number of revolutions of a handle attached to a box. The amount of effort could be changed by a prison warder adjusting the resistance by tightening a screw, the origin of warders becoming known as "screws."

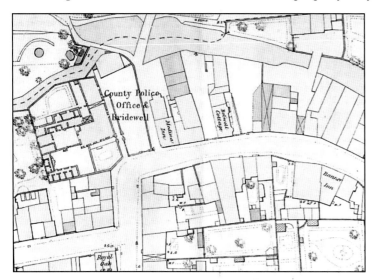

A map showing the new Newport Police Station in 1851, Incorporated into the old Bridewell, opposite what today is the Medina Railway pub. Note what appears to be the segregated cells and an exercise yard.

When Winchester Prison opened, in around 1850, the authorities decided the Newport Bridewell was no longer necessary. Local opposition was outvoted (the Island was, after all, part of Hampshire) and the building was then converted into a borough police station. It remained thus for another forty-five years before Mew Langton's, who had a brewery in nearby Crocker Street, bought and demolished it and constructed a massive malt house on the site in 1898, using Cowes builder James Ball. In November 1979, the building, by this time disused, caught fire and was later demolished. There is now a block of pleasant residential flats on the site, opposite what today is the Medina Railway public house.

The Misses Ashby and their double-fronted shop at the bottom of Holyrood Street.

It was as the Bridewell, however, that rich history was accumulated. It was a temporary home for those awaiting trial at Winchester. One such was Carisbrooke man, John Cockram, who was sentenced to be transported to Australia in 1832 for stealing copper. Lesser offenders included local publican John Bull and his wife, who were in 1817 found guilty of keeping a disorderly house. They were sentenced to three months in the Bridewell, had to pay a 13/4d fine and had their license suspended. In 1820, a young man by the name of Morris, from Shide, was sentenced to serve seven days on the treadmill for refusing to give an oath with respect to a person being intoxicated on the Sabbath. It was where many a petty offender might spend a week following a drunken transgression of the law or where juvenile offenders were whipped. In 1845, Richard Brown, aged 13, and James Booker, who was just 11, broke into Hansen's boatyard at Cowes and stole a quantity of copper. The magistrate gave them one week in the Bridewell, plus a private whipping. Despite having a very high perimeter wall, escapes were not unknown. In 1848, Alexander Ford, a notorious conman, escaped by placing a dummy in his bed, hiding in an empty cell, climbing the high wall and wading through the nearby stream. He hired a pony and trap to take him to Ryde, where he persuaded a boatman to row him across to Portsmouth. From there he made his way first to London and then Hull. The arm of the law stretched a very long way, however, and he was arrested on board a ship that would have taken him overseas, and was returned to the Island. In 1849, what must have been the last escape from the building was made by Henry Groves, of Freshwater, who was charged with sheep stealing. He, too, managed to scale the wall but his suspicious behaviour alerted a rural policeman and he was arrested following a chase, after jumping into a water-filled ditch at Vittlefields.

One Bridewell employee of 1838 sought reinstatement to his job. Frank Webb's titles included those of the 'Beadle, Pounder and Pig Whipper' as well as 'Man and Boy Whipper.' For wielding the cat o' nine tails, he

Mew Langton's malt house under construction in 1899. Health and safety appears to have been less robust than today.

originally received 2/6d, a weekly wage later doubled, and had been employed by the council since 1823. However, the man he asked to speak on his behalf, the superintendent of the watchmen, Mr. Chalk, said if he was compelled to tell the truth, he could only confirm Webb was normally so drunk he often kept him in the watch-house to sober up. Needless to say, the council declined to offer him his job back.

Even as late as 1880, when it was still a police station, punishments were carried out there. James Crews, 15, and his 11-year-old brother, Edward, stole five loaves of bread from a delivery man's cart as he visited houses in East Cowes. The eldest boy was sentenced to one month in prison and his younger brother received six strokes of the birch rod. Eighteen years before that, the Newport to Cowes railway had opened and the street became a main thoroughfare for passengers to and from the station, a move that would have delighted shop owners and publicans alike.

by Alan Stroud

These men and their train are at Freshwater Station sometime in the 1890s. Actually, they are sat in what is now Rapanui's factory just off the roundabout at the bottom of Hooke Hill.

They are the product of that Victorian phenomena, 'railway madness,' a condition that led investors to believe that all they had to do to achieve wealth beyond their wildest dreams was to open a railway between two points. And virtually any two points would do.

The end result was that once upon a time there were over 70 miles of railway lines on the Island. They went everywhere - Cowes to Ryde, Newport to Sandown, Newport to Freshwater and even Brading to Bembridge. However, of all the lines only the Ryde to Ventnor line was ever troubled by making a profit. The others were sorry tales of court battles and bankruptcies, the Newport to Sandown line even collapsing into the arms of the Official Receiver before it was opened. At one point, Parliament even gave permission for a Shanklin to Chale Railway. What a money spinner that would have been. Luckily for us, one by-product of these rash Victorian gambles is that the old lines have left us a network of footpaths and cycleways through some of the loveliest scenery on the Island. That's certainly true of the Freshwater, Yarmouth and Newport Railway.

The line just about managed to break even for most of its life - but only just. It opened in 1889, soldiered on for 64 highly unprofitable years before giving up the ghost and closing in 1953. The line has left its mark, though, and much of it can still be traced today. For example, just a few feet away from the men in the photo, hidden under gardening supplies, is a little known Freshwater secret - in Honnor and Jeffery's yard it is still possible to stand on the original Freshwater station platform! Against all the odds, buried under fence panels and bags of compost, a section of the platform and original station fence has managed to survive. As if that were not enough for train buffs, the cafe next door takes its name from the past, 'The End of The Line'.

The beginning of the line was at Newport railway station which was on Medina Way, roughly where Hamilton and Marshalls the undertakers are. The line then made its way past Sainsbury's filling station, crossed Hunny Hill and then ploughed through Sainsburys frozen vegetable aisle before leaving through the home baking section. It then crossed Petticoat Lane, where the crossing keeper's house still exists, and made its way to Carisbrooke

THE LINE THAT WENT WEST

Station, now buried under the playing fields of Christ The King School in Wellington Road. Passing under the road at Gunville near the Spar store, the line carried on across farmland until it came to Betty Haunt Lane where it passed under the road bridge which still stands to this day, a bridge crossing over a non existent line. For those with eagle eyes, in winter and early spring a crop mark appears across the fields quite clearly showing the line of the long gone track bed.

The next stop was Watchingwell Station; except that it wasn't. The tiny station, which still exists, was solely for the use of the landowner who demanded it as a condition of allowing the line to pass through his land. It can be found on the public footpath that starts at Great Park Farm. Even Calbourne had a station in those days. It was situated along Elm Lane and was demolished in the early seventies. A bungalow, Badger's Bend, now stands on the site and in the private garden at the rear much of the station platform still exists. A mile further on was

The Newport to Freshwater line crossed the road at the bottom of Hunny Hill on this viaduct, seen here in about 1911, The same view, including the very same wall, can be seen today by looking at Hunny Hill from the water feature in Foxes Road, just down from the Sainsburys entrance.

Ningwood Station, at the junction of Wellow Bottom Road and Station Road. Now in private ownership, a surprising amount of the original station still exists. The station building, not open to the public, has become a delightful house and in the back garden a sizeable section of the platforms still exist complete with original platform shelter.

The Yarmouth station building also still exists. After years of stagnation in Council ownership, it was given an imaginative makeover and a new life as the 'Off The Rails' restaurant and cycle hire centre.

Starting from there, the former trackbed to Freshwater forms the cycleway which runs alongside the Yar with beautiful views of the river.

At the end is the picturesque causeway crossing, just down from the Red Lion pub, and from there the trackbed lwends its way through the reed beds back to the 'End Of The Line' café. And all for free.

The original investors in the Freshwater, Yarmouth and Newport Railway might not agree but for us today, their investment was money well spent.

Now buried under the playing fields of Christ The King School in Wellington Road, this is Carisbrooke railway station. Complete with a rarity, a passenger.

DAYS OF INK, BLOTTING PAPER, AND HORLICK'S TABLETS

by Brian Greening

On the basis we inherit many of our characteristics from our parents, when I tell my friends my father was a humble, gentle, quiet, man, and my mother kindness itself, they say I must have been adopted. My father however left me with a few pearls of wisdom when he said such things as: "You will never defeat the system (meaning the establishment) but never, ever give up trying." In addition he told me that "your schooldays will be the best days of your life." I thought about that when I heard recently that more than one hundred and thirty years of local history will end in July, when pupils move from my old school in Barton Road. What will happen to the site is anybody's guess but if past practice is anything to go by, it will become the site for a block of flats.

The school choir, with Ken Clark and Tom Boyland standing on the right Craig Douglas is standing far left, back row.

Having compiled a history of the school, I have become aware of some of the past events that took place there. In the days when boys would walk in from as far away as Wootton Common, around 1925, a pupil turned up wearing a long overcoat that he refused to take off in class. When it was eventually removed, he was found to be minus his trousers, a fact put down to family poverty. Others were known to come to school minus shoes, a fact borne out by a photo I have, taken of a boy in St James's Square watching an Army parade. Parents at Barton at one time refused to send children to school in wet weather because the roads were seas of ankle-deep mud. Then came two world wars and many pupils made the ultimate sacrifice. Older boys than I recall the air-raid shelters on the back sports field that was ploughed up to enable vegetables to be planted to support the war effort. To others the joy of being able to purchase Horlicks tablets, five for a penny, was not forgotten. One good friend recalled his visit to the swimming pool at Seaclose to have his first swimming lesson. He was about to jump in when a warning was sounded of German planes heading up the River Medina from Cowes and the boys all had to dress very quickly. To this day, he still cannot swim and places the blame squarely on Hitler.

The school was renowned for its sporting teams and individuals. A team selected from the pupils who lived in the vicinity of Prospect Road around 1950 would have beaten any other team on the Island. The names of Ash, Strickland, French, Deacon, Perkins and Odell would be heard for years to come in Island football circles, the latter being the late but lovely Bob Odell, who went on to play professionally. Sport is a great means of making lifelong friendships. Many of those friendships that were made when I wore short trousers have endured to this

The boy with no shoes in St James's Square, Newport.

day. I still meet up with four colleagues each week at a local pub where we give a good impersonation of Last of the Summer Wine. The education I received was basic but most of us left school being able to read, write and spell to a reasonable level. We all knew how many furlongs there were to a mile, something that has been an advantage to one of our group, as he is an avid horse-racing fan. He knows the answer, and knows enough letters to write out his betting slip.

Here I want to pay tribute to the teachers of my time, who, in later life, became good friends to many of us. Many of our teachers had returned from war service to take up that bigger challenge of teaching us boys. Fighting Hitler must have been easy compared with trying to keep the gangs of boys from Cross Lane, Royal Exchange and Prospect Road apart at play time. That they did, and that they are recalled with such affection

433	Beard James	22	4	95	12	3	87	John	Royal Exchange.
434	Dibbeck Walter	"	"	"	28	6	87	Robert	Pan Mill.
435	Baker Chas	"	"	"	3	5	88	William	Fairlee
436	Cheverton John	"	"	"	8	5	87	Edmund	31 Crocker St.
437	Attrill Reginald G.	"	"	"	6	3	87	Jesse	4 Fairlee Terrace
438	Martin John S.	"	"	"	28	8	87	John	Cross Lanes
439	Deacon Arthur	"	"	"	13	2	88	Ernest	1 Ash Road. B.V.
440	Cottell Wilfred	"	"	"	26	4	88	George	Cross Lanes
441	Miles J Eli	"	"	"	20	11	88	George Hy	Barton Village
442	Harding Frank	"	"	"	14	9	88	George	10 John Street B.V.
443	Gustar Bertie	"	"	"	19	4	88	Henry	Barton Road.
444	Knight Willie	"	"	"	7	12	87	Tom	26 Coppins Bridge.
445	Jeffry Alfred	"	"	"	22	12	87	Alfred	Barton Village.
446	Hayles Percy	"	"	"	20	7	87	Fred	Victoria Rd. Cross L.
447	White Charles	"	"	"	30	8	88	William	Great Pan Cottages.
448	Hayles Frank	"	"	"	8	6	88	William	Royal Exchange.
449	Kemp Harry	"	"	"	7	2	88	Thomas	4 Victoria Rd. C.L.
450	Pragnell Fred	"	"	"	3	2	88	Ernest	14 Barton Road.
451	Linington Albert	"	"	"	11	2	89	Francis	"Eagle" (P.H.) Cross Lanes.

Barton school register for 1896 showing boys' age of starting school, date of birth, and name of parent and address; all interesting data for researchers.

Former pupil Alan Osborne on a recent return to the school, holding a photo of himself taken 80 years before.

today must say something about their dedication. Bill Milton and David Martin were encountered in later life via their love of cricket, playing for Fairlee and Newport cricket clubs respectively, two men who, when you got to know them, were inspirational. Ralph Lambert I met on several occasions enjoying a cheese scone at the End of the Line Cafe, Freshwater, a man who had seen the wartime beaches of Dunkirk. Jock Ferguson lived near my home in Fairlee Road, while Papa Warder, a dead ringer for Alfred Hitchcock, journeyed each day back to Sandown by train. He seemed so old to us young boys he might have served in the Boer War. It is all so long ago and it seems sad that soon those playgrounds will never again echo to the sound of children's voices.

Let me end by recalling a visit I made to the school a couple of years ago, when I asked the headmistress if she knew why pupils who attended were called Boneheads. She thought it was because the school was built on an old cemetery, something that is not true. The reality came in 1928, when a teacher asked the class what was the shortest verse in the Bible. On getting no response and looking upon a sea of blank faces, he called the boys "numbskulls, thickos, a bunch of Barton Boneheads." Never before had the boys received such a flattering and endearing description, and the name stuck. I might add, the headmistress refused to let me tell her pupils that story, appalled someone could imply they were not bright. For those of less intelligence the shortest verse in the King James Bible is 'Jesus Wept,' John, Chapter 11. The camaraderie that resulted from those years spent sitting at those desks with ink wells and using pens with nibs and sheets of blotting paper still exists today, emphasised by our annual reunion that has been running for thirty four years.

by Alan Stroud

"That the people of Horringford might wish to visit the people of Blackwater was reasonable and proper to suppose, but the railway company could not really expect them to do it often enough to make the line pay" - That was the *Isle of Wight Observer* in 1878, correctly summing up the chances of the newly opened Newport to Sandown railway ever making a profit.

The grandly named Isle of Wight (Newport Junction) Railway was brought into being to link Newport and Sandown via Shide, Blackwater, Merstone, Horringford, Newchurch and Alverstone. The line was opened on a cold February day in 1875 but, and here was the fly in the ointment, only part of it. A massive brick viaduct was required to bring the line into Newport but the cost was way beyond the company's means so for the first few years of operation Shide, not Newport, was where the line began and ended. Not surprisingly, the public did not beat a path to their door and when, after four bad trading years, the company finished the viaduct, the viaduct finished them - not only were the owners' energies spent, so was their cash, and the company collapsed into the arms of the Official Receiver. Under a variety of new owners the line soldiered on.

In 1894, a Newport councillor declared, "If they travelled on the line in a first-class carriage and took a waterproof and umbrella they could travel with fair safety and comfort. The line was a dustbin on wheels (laughter)."

The journey to Sandown began at Newport station, situated in between today's Lidl and Medina Way. It made its way to Coppins Bridge where it crossed over onto the brick viaduct which carried it up past today's cinema complex to run parallel with St George's Way until it reached Shide Station, on the site of what is now the National Tyres depot.

In June 1944, Shide station did its bit for women's lib when 28-year-old Ivy Smith became the first Island railway signalwoman, taking charge of Shide. As the *County Press* pointed out, "The station is no mere railway halt; its working is complicated by a level-crossing on the main Newport-Sandown Road and by considerable

branch line traffic from the nearby Pan chalk pit, which supplies the Medina Cement Mills." Not only did Ivy have to contend with that, she had to open and close the heavy crossing gates, sell and collect tickets, keep the accounts and keep the station clean. In ten busy minutes one summer afternoon, according to the *County Press*, Ivy apparently issued over 50 tickets, opened and closed the level-crossing gates twice, took telephone messages from Newport and Merstone, passed an engine through for Merstone and passed a passenger train for Sandown. She probably broke the land speed record at the same time.

Pan chalk pit lives on as the Shide Quarry Nature Reserve today, where the entrance to the railway tunnel that led from the station siding into the pit can still be seen.

Back at the station, the line crossed the main road onto what is now the cycleway to Merstone and made its way to Blackwater station, which still exists opposite what is now Radcliffe's vegetable shop. Another level crossing took the line across the road and then on to Merstone Junction Station where the lines to Sandown and Ventnor West met. Never quite in the same league as Clapham, the word 'junction' was dropped from the name in later years. Today the station remains as busy as ever as a car park for the users of the cycleway along the old trackbed. The platform still exists in its entirety and in a direct link to the past, the site is still sheltered from the wind by a line of pine trees originally planted by the railway company many years ago.

The next stop was Horringford; the station building still exists at the southern end of Arreton main road. At Newchurch all trace of the station has disappeared, a bungalow sitting in its place at the bottom of the Shute. The next station, Alverstone, still sits in the middle of the village. It has recently been lovingly and sensitively restored by its owners and today all that is missing is a train. The cycleway carries on along the track but doesn't quite make its way to Sandown, instead, petering out alongside the Fairway caravan park just off Perowne Way.

In 1956, after 80 loss making years, the line was closed by British Railways. The closure came as no surprise and was accompanied by very little protest. The motor car and buses had won the day and in an ironic twist made it possible for the bicycle to take over from steam. "All change," as they say.

Shide railway station in the late 1890s, complete with advertising hoardings and flower beds on the platform. All that's missing is Will Hay.

THE UNSEEMLY BATTLE FOR BROOK GREEN

by Brian Greening

In all families there are incidents that occur that in later years are not always brought up in company. In the local Pittis family it was the event that we might call "The Battle for Brook Green," that caused them some embarrassment. It was finally resolved in 1822 at Winchester Assizes over the validity of a will and the eventual ownership of that estate on the Isle of Wight. It was an action for 'ejectment' to recover two parts of that estate known as Brook Green under the will of a James Stephens. The property was valued at around £8,000, a not insubstantial sum at that time. Mr. Stephens had been a wealthy, albeit eccentric, farmer and the proprietor of Brook Green who died in June 1819. At the time of his death, he had three married nieces of whom he had been extremely fond. They were a Mrs. Rogers, a Mrs. Browning and the third had married Mr. John Pittis. Besides these three beneficiaries, Mr. Stephens had a female servant who had served him well for nearly forty years as a housekeeper. In July 1814, Mr. Stephens had made his first will, dividing his property between his three nieces, excepting that he gave to his housekeeper a cottage and furniture on the estate and an annuity of £50 a year. When Mr. Stephens finally died, his 1814 will was read at his funeral but Mr. Edward Pittis, brother of Mr. John Pittis, who was by then in America, stepped forward and produced a will dated 1817, in which everything had been left to Mrs. John Pittis, one of the nieces, to the exclusion of the two other ladies and the housekeeper was only given an annuity. A second paper he produced gave him, Edward Pittis, power of attorney, empowering him to take possession of, and have passed to him, all rents due. The question to be decided was the validity of the 1817 will.

There were many witnesses produced by both sides. One was a Mr. Griffiths who had been Mr. John Pittis solicitor for fourteen years and who recalled him coming into his office and asking him to draw up, within one hour, a will that he dictated. While the solicitor and later the judge felt it was unusual for one man to draw up another man's will to be signed, the attorney recalled that he did it reluctantly as he had acted for Mr. Pittis for many years. Other witnesses included three employees of Mr. Pittis, namely Futcher, Whittington and Young, who gave evidence of being taken by John Pittis to Mr. Stephens's house in 1817 and acting as witnesses to Mr. Stephens's signature. This was a case that raised great interest locally and after an all-day trial in front of what was called a special jury, they returned an almost instantaneous verdict in favour of Mrs. Browning, Mrs. Robinson and the housekeeper. The report ended by saying these ladies returned home in a horse-drawn carriage decorated with flags.

John Pittis, as earlier mentioned had emigrated by then to America for in 1819 he had hired a ship and set off for Baltimore. Indeed, an article in *The Salisbury and Winchester Journal* for May 1819 records as follows: "A fine brig, of 500 tons burden, called the Resolution, Capt J. R. Clarke, master, sailed on Sunday morning last from Cowes, in the Isle of Wight, for Baltimore. She had on board about fifty passengers, for whom excellent accommodations were provided for the voyage. This vessel was chartered by Mr. John Pittis, of Newport, for himself and family." It was later disclosed that the reasons John Pittis had emigrated were variously described as "through embarrassment and distress." Whether this was financial, matrimonial or for that matter some other reason we do not learn. We do know that when John made that trip with his pregnant wife they took with them eight children, two others having died at a young age and who were buried on the Isle of Wight. They also took

A typical pioneer family in America.

Brook Green in 2019, a scene little changed in 100 years.

with them their household effects, horses, chickens, gold and fourteen boys to help with the work, these boys possibly being recruited from the Workhouse. They landed in Baltimore two months later and then set off like a Wild West covered wagon convoy to eventually settle in a place called Brownsville in Ohio.

Letter from America.

Following John Pittis's journey to America in 1819, we learn a little of his success in an extract from a letter sent back to a Mr Urry in April 1822 from James Abraham, who had been a respectable miller on the Island before he too went to America, where he married Sarah Pittis, one of the daughters. He states, *"If you will come here you will do well. You can do almost any kind of farming and here even an old woman can farm. Here we make soap and candles, we make and sell beer without a licence. Bread is cheap and good. A farmer may raise all kinds of grain, hops, tobacco and grapes by the bushel. Poultry is abundant, hens' eggs are plentiful, and people think nothing of keeping over one hundred hens. I believe Mr. Pittis has three hundred. There is plenty of milk and the countryside is full of pheasants, partridges, deer, wild turkeys and pigeons by the thousands. Hogs are cheap and salt is around 4/6d a bushel. I have sixty-five acres of land, thirty of them cleared, with two good houses, a barn, two stables, and other outbuildings. We have a good coal bank, and a sugar camp, which makes me £500 a year. There is also a fine spring of water not to be equalled by the Carisbrooke springs."*

I would stress here the Pittis family in general served the Island well and their most famous member, Sir Francis Pittis, was not only mayor of Newport on eight occasions, but he was also knighted by Queen Victoria.

Sir Francis Pittis.

"FRESHWATER - AS TAWDRY AND SLUTTISH AS AN UNSWEPT ROOM"

by Alan Stroud

The title is not my words, but those of writer Aubrey de Selincourt in his 1948 travel book 'The Isle of Wight.' The full quote, in all its splendid glory, reads : "It is better to travel than to arrive. I wish the saying were not true of Freshwater Bay. This famous beauty spot is as tawdry and sluttish as an unswept room. The dismal hotels, the dreary eating-houses, the neglected shanties, the cracked concrete, the heaped stones, the patient charabancs, the pervading atmosphere of paper-baggery and crumbs, are disconcerting to say the least of it. Being hungry, I entered one of the eating houses - I hoped at least for a paste sandwich or a sawdust bun. But there was nothing. I escaped as quickly as I could to Tennyson Down..."

Freshwater wasn't the only place to get a going over from Aubrey. He detected ghastly horridness everywhere he looked. "I was soon in Wroxall, perhaps too soon, for the village is of an indescribable, stony-hearted ugliness... From the quay, Newport looks its worst... Attached to the inn at Downend is a large and dreadful road-house... There are no slums or squalor at Upper Ventnor, only downright savage ugliness.... One wants one's blind eye at Brighstone to remove the blemishes; the church hall, the asbestos tea gardens. It was said to me that all the village wanted now was a nice public lavatory - on the model, I suppose, of the cinema at Newport."

Moving swiftly on, in 1918 Britain had been at war for four years. Rationing was in place and German U-boats were having great success sinking convoys carrying much needed food from America. In March a U.S. ship, the War Knight, was bound for London with a cargo of bacon, lard, flour and rubber. Just after midnight on March 24th she collided with a fuel tanker in Sandown Bay. Both vessels were drenched in fuel oil which then burst into flames and the massive explosion killed 36 of her crew. The blazing War Knight was towed to Freshwater Bay where she had even more bad luck when she struck a mine. To put out the fire she was sunk by torpedo and cannon and as she sank her cargo spilled into the sea, eventually finding its way onto the beach where hungry locals did their best to remove the unexpected windfall before the Customs men arrived. By the time they did

The Toogood family have been professionally photographers of the West Wight for over 100 years. The photographs on these two pages are taken from their original glass negatives. This is Freshwater Bay in the 1930s and inset is 'Arch Rock' which stood just behind where the photograph was taken from. In October 1992 it collapsed into the sea.

arrive, most of the bounty had been 'liberated' so house-to-house searches were mounted, resulting in 38 prosecutions for stealing contraband. The cases were all heard on the same day, the train carrying them to Newport being referred to as the 'Bacon and Lard Special.' The prosecutions were seen as mean spirited and caused a great deal of bad feeling. There were several who had removed industrial amounts of pork and lard from the beach by lorry but they somehow escaped prosecution, leading many in court to protest that the authorities had "found the sprats and let the whales go free." It was to no avail. They were all found guilty and fined from £1 to £5, hefty amounts for village workers. The next week, 'W.H' wrote to the *County Press:* "Sir, The pieces of pork in question were smothered with black grease from the burning ship, and with sand and seaweed added to the grease, some of it looked quite unfit for human food. The people who took it to their homes and cleaned it deserved credit instead of punishment, in trying to save food which otherwise would have perished on the shore where scores of pieces are now rotting and being devoured by seagulls." The *County Press* agreed that justice had not been seen to be done: "In these days of food shortages the public should be encouraged in salving every possible ounce of food."

The War Knight ablaze, March 1918.

The War Knight is still making its presence felt. Bales of rubber from her cargo came ashore at Freshwater Bay in 1994 and again in 2011, and today the wreck, 15 metres deep, is a popular diving site.

In the early 1980s, Colin Fairweather and I recorded interviews with people in their 70s and 80s, recording their way of life in the early years of the last century (the interviews are in our book *Island Lives*.) One of the subjects was Will Cassell, a man who spent his entire life in Hulverstone village. We asked him about the War Knight ... "Ah, yes. That was Palm Sunday night that was, and up at Hulverstone we could see the smoke and as it got dusk we could see the the flames, and she came in there right under Freshwater Bay, you see. She was loaded up with all sorts of different farm machinery but it was all smashed up. And she was loaded up with food, bacon, pork and lard, and after about three days a lot of this come ashore, you see, and from Freshwater Bay to Chale the beach was littered with hams, pork and boxes of lard and one night me father and me, we went down on the beach there and I think it was ten hams we picked up. We washed 'em off and we took 'em up home. We put 'em up in the horse stable loft and buried 'em under the hay 'cause the Customs blokes come round, you see, and if they found anybody with any hams, or meat or anything, they summonsed them, and the bloke that kept the pub, they went there and found he had some and he was fined three pounds. Everybody round about had some, yes. When she finally sunk down you could see the two funnels and a bit of the mast for years afterwards."

Freshwater Bay in the 1930s, with the remains of 'Arch Rock' in the distance.

by Brian Greening

Readers must get fed up with me "banging on" about the shops of yesteryear but for me they existed in my youth, a period I look back on with many happy memories. Each shop specialized in a certain range of products meaning the weekly shop took in up to a dozen different shops. Cigarettes were bought at one of five of W.J. Ruggs tobacconists in the town. Our newspaper, the Daily Herald, was bought in Mr. Hancock's tiny shop in Pyle Street, close to St James's Square. For our groceries, I would be sent with a long list to Lipton's in the High Street, where all my purchases would be placed in a free brown paper carrier bag with string for handles. By the time I had staggered home, my fingers were virtually bloodless. I went to Downer's the butchers in Lower St James's Street to buy my father's chitterlings, his treat each Friday that he smothered in mustard, one of only a couple of shops I could still patronise today. Fruit and vegetables were obtained from either Salter's or Daish's, that were opposite what once was the Medina Cinema, and cakes came from the nearby, never to be forgotten, Medina Cafe. For bread, I was always sent to Perkins shop below County Hall, close to one of several sub post offices around the town, this one being part of Mr. Dore's grocery shop. The other thing that added to the pleasure of shopping was the personal service, a chat and a smile from owners who, in some cases, lived on the premises. Of course, for today's shoppers there are advantages and disadvantages. Shopping is all under one roof, but that roof may be out of town.

Spanners shop in Newport High Street in the 1970s

I pondered both the changes in my lifetime, and the Newport High Street of 1851, aided by that year's census return. One of the main observations was just how many of the shop owners and their families lived over their premises. Not only did they live there but so did their employees and their domestic staff, and nursemaids, to help with the children. Of course, not every house had a shop below, but those that did were generally fine buildings, only afforded by the wealthy and persons of status; men who used the census return to tell us more about themselves. For example, many of the members of Newport's borough council at that time lived in the High Street. Men from the Mew, Wavell, Pring, Sayer, Pinhorn and Pinnock families were all town councillors. At No. 8 High Street lived Thomas Cooke, who told us on the census form that he was a landed proprietor and a magistrate. Although there was only his wife and himself, he had four elderly, unmarried servants living in his

Butcher Harry Pitcher's shop in Pyle Street.

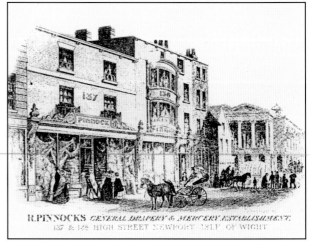

Robert Pinnock was Mayor of Newport on five occasions, dying in 1887.

house. Edward Caplin was a silk mercer, a person who dealt in cottons, linens and woollen clothes. Caplin employed three assistants and an apprentice, all of whom, with Celia Kirsley, a servant, lived beneath his roof. Edward Pinnock was a draper who, beside his wife and four children, had four draper's assistants, an apprentice, and three servants. This pattern of employees and domestic staff 'living in' was common to the High Street, where houses were generally large and even if residents never had a shop beneath their premises, they were often employers of labour within the town. Robert Stratton was only 24, but stated he was a builder who employed seventeen men. His brother was an architect and surveyor.

Coach proprietor, William Lambert, employed eighteen people and lived two doors away from a man with a name and initials familiar to most on the Island. This was Mr. H. W. Morey, aged at the time just 35, and a builder who employed nine people. It would be a very big coincidence if this was not the man who founded the large timber business. One family that was in Newport High Street for more than 130 years were the Millidges, chemists who stayed in the same premises for all that time. Richard Pittis, a member of an Island family that can be traced back to 1480, was at this time a High Street grocer and wine merchant. At the Bugle Hotel things were not looking too good, for on the night the census was taken, they had a solitary guest, a man who gave his trade as that of a 'nail master.' The business was listed as having a barmaid, porter, chambermaid, cook, scullery maid and housemaid, all living in.

Jukes, in St Thomas Square, that indispensable hardware shop.

One person is a complete mystery however, and this was Eliza Hopkins, who described herself as a lace manufacturer employing no less than 40 women but she does not record any of these living with her. Was she simply a supervisor at Nunn's lace factory at Staplers, or was she outsourcing work to her employees in their homes? One popular trade was that of boot and shoemaker, and repairer, in the days when people had their footwear mended. One such shoemaker was John Milligan. Another oft repeated description in the census was 'annuitant' which was applied to elderly ladies who were in lodgings. This usually meant they had an additional income from savings or property. For many years, family businesses in Newport became established and survived for well over 100 years, such as Alderslades, Snellgroves, Jukes, Wadhams, Millidge, Jordan and Stanley, Whitchers, Upward and Rich, as well as solicitors such as Eldridge, Roach Pittis and Buckell. All these premises made their customers and clients feel like old friends and offered full-time employment. Today, national retailers rarely offer full-time jobs, employing staff on an almost weekly basis on zero hour contracts that mean an employee never knows from week to week whether he will have a wage packet each week. Twenty years plus service under those terms as happened in the past will never happen again. I wrote a book once called 'We Have Lived Through the Best Years'. I never said a truer word.

John Sheath, often considered a rival to Guys shop, in Pyle Street, now a Mc Donalds.

BEER, BLOATERS AND THE MOST SENSIBLEST MAN IN THE WORLD

by Alan Stroud

Times may change but human nature doesn't. Proving the point, here are some court cases from over 100 years ago involving the Crown v. Alcohol. Then, as now, there was only ever going to be one winner....

In September 1889, James Gustar, a Cowes butcher, was charged with running an unlicenced slaughterhouse.... In court all was well until 'Moth, the slaughterman' took the stand to give evidence on Gustar's behalf. As the *County Press* put it, "He saluted the Bench, wished them a happy new year, hoped they long might reign, and desired to know what they wanted of him. Taking up the Bible he expressed a love for it and said he meant to give it a good long kiss – which he proceeded to do. – He was ordered to stand down as "too tipsy to give evidence", which he did, after saluting the Bench with comic gravity." Mr Gustar was fined £5.

The Victoria Inn, on Snooks Hill, seen here in the 1890s. The pub closed its doors in the mid-1920s and in the 1950s became Vic Clark's 'Gents Hairdressers'. The building was demolished in the 1970s to make way for the wonderful Coppins Bridge roundabout. Readers of a certain age will also remember the 'Lucky Dip' a few doors down.

When Henry Wolfe tried to sell fish to Christmas shoppers in Ryde High Street in 1902 he ended up charged with loitering on the footway. P.C. Denness told the court that on the evening of 20th of December, Henry was in the street with a crowd around him. "He was the worse for drink and was singing and calling attention to his show in language which was not very choice, calling out 'What do you think of my — show?' I told him he was blocking the street but he replied that he was the boss and should do what he liked. He then held up a herring and shouted 'Who will give me a penny for this?' He then got some bloaters and threw them about for people to scramble for and he was not particular whose face he threw them into. I said, 'You are acting very foolishly, Wolfe, and will get yourself into trouble'. He replied 'When you are talking to me you are talking to the most sensiblest man in the world' (laughter)." Henry took the stand and agreed that he "might have had a glass" and that he had five previous convictions. Now he had six - he was found guilty and fined ten shillings.

In 1912 Edward Groves, a labourer of East Cowes, was charged with disorderly behaviour. He arrived at court drunk. "Defendant (shouting): I am not drunk, sir. I guarantee I am not. Did you ever see a man drunk standing as I am. I can stand on my head (laughter). A drunken man cannot stand the same as a mackerel (laughter). I like a mackerel when he is fresh. I am an honest man. Look at my honest blue eyes (laughter). – Supt Galloway (to the sergeant) : Take him out and charge him with being drunk and disorderly."

In July 1907, Margaret Chambers, "a married woman of Cowes," was charged with being drunk and disorderly. She told the magistrates, "I dare say it is right, sir. I take fits now and then - fits of drunkenness' (laughter). P.C. Chisholm said he saw her drunk, lying on the ground for 20 minutes and using the most disgusting language he had ever heard. The Chairman: Margaret Chambers, the Bench sentence you to be imprisoned with hard labour for seven days. Defendant: A good job. Ain't I glad – Chambers refused to leave the dock and was removed by several policemen, who carried her out of the Court screaming."

The Prince of Wales pub in Ryde High Street, seen in about 1910. The pub closed in the 1980s and the frontage was rebuilt, retaining much of the look of the original pub. Edward VII, who the pub was named after, was a lover of the racecourse and would no doubt appreciate the fact that it is currently home to the bookies 'Betfred'.

The New Inn at the junction of Cowes High Street and The Cut. It closed in the late 1960s, standing empty until it was demolished in 1980. The Day Lewis pharmacy now occupies the site.

In 1908, Frank Dore of Elmfield, was summoned for drunk and disorderly behaviour... "When defendant's name was called he shouted from the back of the Court 'I am here, but I can't get up to the box'. He was brought up by a constable and shouted 'Not guilty' in a loud voice. He was told that he must behave himself. He swore that he was innocent, and at this a man at the back of the Court called 'Hear, hear' and had to be ejected. Defendant was fined five shillings and then William Tutton, the man who had been ejected, took the stand. Tutton smiled and nodded to the magistrates. The Clerk asked : Is he drunk? - P.C. Broome: Not yet, Sir (laughter). Defendant was charged with having being drunk on the 12th inst., and replied 'That's bad, ain't it? (laughter) A drunken man gets sober sometimes, but a fool never gets wise' (much laughter). Defendant kept up a running commentary while the evidence was being given, and said to the Chairman 'You've knowed me a good many years, ain't you?' (laughter). When sentenced to pay 2s.6d., he observed to one of the magistrates 'Ain't your head going grey; what have you been doing to it?' He was removed from the dock and left the Court apparently very well pleased with himself."

THE CHARACTERS WHO BRIGHTENED OUR DAYS

by Brian Greening

I often bemoan the demise of the old-time characters, who made life that bit more colourful. They were part of the town's fabric and known to the majority of local inhabitants. In a previous article, I referred to Uriah Guy, who frequented the town quay, and was alleged to be the source of what was the equivalent of Viagra in those days. He nearly lost his life, however, as he sold several to the skipper of a Poole bound ship with instructions to take one only when approaching Poole harbour. The Captain could not resist taking one half-way home and spent the next day sitting on the loo. Apparently the tablets were laxative pills. When the skipper next returned he was looking for Uriah who had to go into hiding.

My good friend Bill Shepard recalled Peewit Grimes, a man who drove one of the old time steam engines years ago. Upon seeing a pretty girl, Mr. Grimes would give a toot on his steam whistle. It sounded like the word "peewit," hence the nickname that stayed with him all his life. Another man went door-to-door selling watercress and he naturally earned the name Freddy Watercress. Two men would compete for custom at Newport Railway Station to deliver parcels to shops in the town. They often ended having a slanging match and appeared to spend their meagre earnings in a pub, hence their names Beery Manhole and Beery Mathews.

In more recent times, we had Theodore, who I always felt was unfairly described as a tramp, a man who would play the piano, often at The Horseshoe, Northwood. He ended his days at Ryde, where he slept rough in Appley Woods but sadly died on the mainland in January 1987. His ashes were scattered at Yeovil crematorium.

Another character who emerged in the fifties was Nobber Knowles, a coal delivery man who in his prime had been a footballer with a fearsome reputation. He took part in a football match at St. Swithins approved school one Saturday at Yarmouth and during the game he resorted to unfair tactics to thwart the opposition. After the game, the Catholic brothers always invited teams back for tea and biscuits and said a few complimentary words about the game. On this occasion, however, Brother Cassian must have been incensed with Nobber's play, as he stated "there were twenty one gentlemen on the field that day and one 'blackguard'". Later, Nobber took to refereeing and sometimes acted as linesman for Newport FC at Church Litten. As soon as the opposition crossed the half-way line, up went Nobber's flag for offside. Most referees soon learned to ignore his dodgy calls and with this, Nobber would stick his flag in the ground and depart the field of play. Nobber was, however, a very generous man. He was always ready to help a needy cause and he was one of the instigators of the annual Steak v. Butter football matches that raised money for the Home for the Blind at Polars. The steak team was chosen from butchers, while the butter team consisted of grocers. And these games were certainly competitive. Each year a celebrity was invited to commence the game with a ceremonial 'kick off'. I recall one year it was a man called Charles Hill, who became a member of parliament. From 1942, he gave advice each morning to the listening

Theodore, who played the piano, in more recent times

Nobber Knowles, right, receiving a cheque for the Home for the Blind from Mr. Arnold the owner of Arnold's fair that visited each year..

Harry Orchard, double amputee, who sold matches and shoe laces outside Newport post office

public on how to maintain good health. This was before television was popular and it could be disconcerting to hear him on the radio around 8.15 am while we were sitting at the breakfast table, giving his recommendations for curing piles and constipation. Advertising restrictions meant he could not divulge his full name, so he simply became known as the 'Radio Doctor'. After a long and varied career as an MP, he was sacked by Harold Macmillan in a Tory purge in 1962.

Another celebrity to kick off the annual football match was Bruce Seton who, after a notable army career that included service in the Black Watch, went into acting and films. His most notable success, however, came from starring as 'Fabian of Scotland Yard', which became a TV favourite of the day.

One of the most popular stars to undertake the commencement of the game was Newport's Carnival Queen in 1951, Jean Hendey. She made such an impression on the *County Press* cartoonist, Tom Smitch, that he penned one

Stanley Stevens 'steak v. butter' carnival entry c. 1955

of her undertaking the task (see opposite). Jean Hendey, I am pleased to say, is still alive and still kicking, although probably not footballs any more, and lives at Sandown. Among those who took part in these games were employees of Stanley Stevens, the well-known and sometimes controversial local butcher, members of the Wray grocery family, the butchering Barton brothers, and a man I used to have lunch with most Sundays, sadly the late Roger Cross, who was employed in Ken Miller's grocery shop at the top of Newport High Street, (for which in my opinion he deserves the Victoria Cross). Nobber Knowles in his usual impartial way often refereed these games, to which supporters were attracted in great numbers. Today, there are hardly enough independent butchers and grocers for a doubles tennis match, a sure sign of how times have changed.

Poster for the Steak v. Butter football match

Tom and Emma Beard.

I cannot end without mentioning brother and sister, Tom and Emma Beard (seen opposite) who lived in South Street. They had an old gramophone that they would place on the pavement outside their house and play records, mainly of hymns. For years Tom pushed Emma around in a wheelchair but the story goes that Tom eventually had to take to that form of transport himself so Emma simply vacated the seat and pushed him around. Great memories of local characters who were harmless and brought a little colour to the town.

The Christmas Card And The 'Troublesome Photograph'

by Alan Stroud

It's a cold January evening in 1909 and Annie Keen, the heavily pregnant landlady of the Crown Hotel, Ryde, is standing in the entrance hall talking to a man. He is a plain-clothes policeman who has come to discuss her husband's arrest earlier that afternoon. As they talk, a man comes in from the street and approaches them. He takes a revolver from his pocket and shoots Mrs Keen at point-blank range. She cries "Oh God," and collapses into the arms of the policeman.

The policeman, P.C. Fewtrell, laid Mrs Keen on the floor in the passage. She was bleeding and her dress around the bullet hole was on fire. Fewtrell put the flames out and then arrested the man with the gun, William Yardley, who had already been seized by customers.

The scene was described in more detail by P.C. Fewtrell at Yardley's trial, "When he shot her he said 'There, you bitch!' and threw the revolver on the ground saying, 'I've finished. He has advertised me for the last fortnight, and now I'll advertise the Crown Hotel.' Mrs Keen threw up her arms and said, "Oh God." I caught her and said to Yardley, 'Stop! That is enough, Mr. Yardley'. I later cautioned him and he said 'Oh God! What made

The Crown Hotel and adjacent Lounge in the 1950s

me do it? I had no intention of doing it when I came to Ryde this morning'. He kept muttering about the Crown Hotel - the Crown Hotel had ruined him."

The news of the shooting spread quickly and St Thomas Square was soon packed with a dense crowd who booed and hissed Yardley when he was brought out to a carriage. Mrs. Keen was taken to Ryde hospital where it was found that by a stroke of luck the bullet had been deflected by her ribs and it was safely removed. Shaken by events, Mrs Keen gave birth the next day to a premature but healthy girl. The shooting caused a sensation and was reported in newspapers as far away as Exeter and Dundee. The *County Press* knew more than it was prepared to tell at this point, saying, "As usual in all such cases, many sensational rumours are current in the town. Most of these deal with matters which it would not be proper to discuss here."

It wasn't long though before the matters were discussed freely. Just eight weeks later, not only Yardley but also Mrs Keen's husband, James, appeared in court. Yardley had attempted suicide the night before and appeared in the dock, with his head bandaged, to face charges of shooting with intent to murder, and Mr Keen was accused of threatening to kill Yardley. Both cases were heard on the same day, the judge wanting to hear the jury's verdict on the first case before pronouncing sentence in the other.

The *Portsmouth Evening News* reported, "Ryde Shooting Sensation. Photograph Caused Trouble." Indeed it did. In the crowded courtroom, all was revealed. The Keens had met the Yardleys seven years before, at Aldershot army barracks, when both husbands were stationed there. They were all on friendly terms. In the intervening years Keen had taken on the Crown while Yardley had remained in the army. All was well until a Christmas card arrived at the Crown. Inside was a photograph of Yardley and his family, including his daughter. In court, Keen's solicitor asked Mrs Keen, "Some unpleasantness arose in consequence of the photograph? – Yes." Mr Keen then took the stand and told the court that his wife and the Yardleys were great friends but he (Keen) was always reserved. Q. Why? On account of Yardley's marked affection for my wife. Q. Your wife had a child Maisie in 1904. Did you have any idea in your head about that child? Yes, its paternity - from the moment of the birth. Q. Did you suspect anyone? It came into my mind, but out of respect for my wife I discounted it. Q. When you saw that photograph did something strike you? Instantly. There was a child there which I thought for a moment was Maisie, my daughter. There was a waitress standing alongside, Edith Whitford, and I said to her, "Who is that child like?" She said "Maisie." I went to bed but lay awake all night thinking. Q. Your wife heard the remark? Yes. I spoke to her but I wasn't satisfied with her answer. I spoke to her again and she made a statement to me. Q. What was the effect upon you? Broken hearted, downhearted, nothing else in the world to live for, when I found my wife had been betrayed by a comrade. Q. You are usually a sober man. Were you at this time? No, I took to drink. Until I had the letters I wrote read back to me I had no idea of what was in them. Q. Did you write, "I will either shoot him like a dog or crush him to pulp? It says so…. I can remember faintly writing letters but I am not clear as to what was in them."

Keen's letters, sad and often incoherent, were read to the Court. In one he told Yardley that he would 'kill him like a dog' when he saw him. As a result Yardley went to the police and Keen was arrested. He asked P.C. Fewtrell to take a message to his wife and it was at that point that Yardley had entered the Crown and shot Annie Keen.

The *Isle of Wight Observer* reported, "Mr Keen's solicitor said the case was one of the most terrible human dramas the court had had to deal with. He was going to ask the jury to say that when the prisoner wrote those wild incoherent letters he was suffering from one of the greatest mental shocks a man could have experienced."

A horse and cart outside the Crown Hotel Lounge in the 1910s

His speech obviously had the desired effect and the jury returned a verdict of not guilty which was greeted by loud applause in the packed court room. Then it was Yardley's turn in the dock. He told the court he carried a pistol after receiving the threatening letters; "I went into the Hotel and saw P.C. Fewtrell in plain clothes. I confused the idea of the constable being there with Keen being there and took out the pistol to move it to another pocket, and my horror it went off." The jury were not convinced by Yardley's explanation and found him guilty of shooting with intent to kill. He was sentenced to ten years hard labour.

And there the matter might have rested except that five years later Mr Keen divorced his wife, when even more details were revealed. The *Isle of Wight Observer* reported, "Mr Keen noticed the resemblance of one of Yardley's children to one of his, and his wife then admitted that the child was hers, and it was born while he was serving in South Africa. In a letter to her husband, Mrs Keen had written:- "You say you never could live with me again. Oh, Jim, how sorry I am. I have been living in hope, and praying that one day we shall be happy again. Now I know it cannot be. I would be the happiest woman in the world if I could blot out these years, instead of which I know there is not a more wretched creature living. Night and day it is forever in my thoughts. Oh, how happy I once was. And now think what I am. Heaven knows I never meant to do wrong. When I think of the old days and what a happy existence we had, the agony comes on, and so it will always be. There are only two things for me to do, either to go to Canada and start a new life, or take my own life, which is a worthless one. I know that you are always good. I have killed every liking you had for me, and only hatred remains. I do not think a woman ever paid more for anything than myself. I know you will always look after the children, only do not make them hate me. Whatever comes to me serves me right. There are heaps of good women, but I happen to be a bad one. I never dreamt that it would ever mean our parting."

The divorce was granted. It was a sad end to a sad case.

Crown Hotel, Ryde, I.W.
Please pass the word onto Liverpool and anywhere else also. I trust in your kindness to him that he has not betrayed you, the ——. God have mercy upon ourselves when we meet face-to-face, man to man. I will either shoot him dead like a dog or crush him to pulp. I will damn him to the whole regiment, to his comrades, to his wife, to his children, to his officers, to his officers' wives, to his battery comrades' wives, to the Aldershot command. If he lives to go to India I will damn him there, and to his children in years to come. I cannot even spare in my wrath even the grave of his departed child shall crumble his feet at my mercy (sic). He is the most deceitful and detestful man in the regiment, despised by officers, by NCO's, and by his men, known through the regiment as a dirty cur. What price his bones when I have finished with him in the Barracks at Aldershot – the Barracks I love so well, the men I love so well and have their respect. There is one I hope to spare, his wife, in the drama, or is it comedy, or farce, or tragedy. I am sure I do not know, but the sins of the father shall be born unto the children, even unto the third and fourth generation. Vengeance is mine, I will repay, sayeth the Lord. My brain is dizzy. I have this pen in hand. I was elsewhere 22 years ago; I enlisted as a private soldier, penniless. Since that I have had to keep my father and mother, my wife, my five children and Bradley's —— and I have saved sufficient money to come into the smartest house in the Isle of Wight – a free house, and the customers love me, but I am dead to them - dead to the world. I have no wife, no children, nothing but death for me, thanks to Bradley's lust and his love for another woman and entirely forgetting his own lady, God bless her! God have mercy on his soul. My brain is dizzy. What will you give for his broken bones when I have finished with him … After you receive this drop me a line of sympathy. I have one ambition in life and that is to be a man and a gentleman, though once a private soldier. Death where is thy sting. If your wife has escaped from his penance you have something to be thankful for, for he is ashamed of his wife and her family.

One of the letters produced in court that Keen had written to William Yardley.

by Brian Greening

After the end of the First World War the Island took every opportunity to celebrate just about anything after the grim reality of the preceding years. Locally, one group who suffered tremendous losses was the Isle of Wight Rifles, at Gallipoli, the roll-call of the dead and injured illustrating war is no discriminator between rich and poor. The disparate nature of those who gave their lives is illustrated by the memorial stone to former pupils of my old school at Barton who were killed in the same conflict, as was the son of the wealthy Island benefactor, Sir Charles Seely. After the end of that awful conflict, the community which had lost its fathers and sons, looked forward to a bright future and took the opportunity to do so using one of the tools of war, a tank.

'Winifred' the tank makes her way down Hunnyhill after her 2 mph journey from Cowes.

From October 1917, every town with a population of more than 10,000 was asked to send a weekly sum from its area equal to ten shillings (50p) per head. By January 1919, the *County Press* reported that Newport had raised a staggering £408,593, an average of almost £6,000 a week. It was raised by numerous small groups, including the Women's Association, the St Paul's Association, the James Thomas Association, (a named casualty of the war) and the IW Central Railway Association plus the local Oddfellows. Many schools, too, helped contribute, including those at Shorwell, Chillerton and Arreton. The headmaster of Barton School, Skipper Ouseley, was later awarded the M.B.E. for being the leading organiser of this fundraising task.

The tank had first to be brought from the mainland, a task achieved not without difficulty. Once on the Island

Island servicemen, the IW Knuts.

it clanked its way from Cowes at around 2mph to Newport where it descended Hunnyhill. It then made its way to Quay Street where, for the rest of the morning, fascinated crowds, made up of numerous schoolchildren, gazed

A British tank at the Battle of Cambrai, 1917.

at it in awe. It should be remembered that in the First World War tanks were a new innovation and so quite a novelty to the public, most never having seen one before. In the afternoon, the tank was driven up Carisbrooke Mall and down Recreation Ground Road, where the bridge in the road leading to the ground had to be strengthened to enable it to cross the Lukely stream before turning into Priory fields, the gateway to the sports ground proving too difficult to negotiate. Eventually, it made its way to its final resting place in the far corner of the ground.

In September 1919 there was a grand ceremony held in Newport's Victoria Recreation Ground with the official handing-over to the town of a tank with an interesting tale. The tank was 26ft long, 13ft wide and more than 9ft tall, weighing around 27 tons. On the day the tank was presented to Newport, bullet holes could still be seen in its armour. Local dignitaries were told by the army personnel attending that tanks of that type were always known as either male or female and their tank was the smaller Mark IV "female," that carried six Lewis guns and 24,000 rounds of ammunition.

It had seen action at the Battle of Cambrai in November and December of 1917. Cambrai was an important town as it contained a large strategic railhead and in front of it lay the strong Hindenburg Line, a defensive position in which the Germans placed great faith. Four hundred and seventy-six tanks, including their tank advanced on a ten kilometer front at enemy positions and the Germans were driven back. Eight thousand prisoners were taken and a great deal of enemy armaments were captured.

When Lt Roberts performed the handing-over ceremony, smashing a bottle of champagne on the steel, he named her Winifred, after Newport's lady mayoress, Mrs Winifred Whitcher. Note. At Ryde their tank was also given a lady's name, possibly after of one of their notable citizens.

Temporary graves of Island servicemen at Gaza

Among the other civic leaders in attendance at Newport were Mayor Whitcher, Mr Millgate, Councillors Quinton, Rugg, Deacon, Wadham, A. E. Harvey and Skipper Ouseley. The boy scouts formed a guard of honour while the girl guides and the St Paul's and town bands added to the pageant. When I made inquiries of people who might have seen the tank, former Barton School pupil, sadly now the late, Peter Meech, recalled as a young boy sitting on it and watching a first-class cricket match at the recreation ground between Hampshire and Middlesex in 1938. It was, he claimed, certainly still there after the Second World War.

Isle of Wight Rifles bugle practice.

by Alan Stroud

In an interview with Alan and Tom Stroud, Ray Foulk, organiser of the original Isle of Wight Festival told the story of staging the first event in 1968. "There was quite a team of us, but primarily it was my brother Ronnie and I who spearheaded the thing. I had worked at the *County Press* on a five-year apprenticeship and left there at 21,

just 18 months earlier, to set up my own printing business and I was running it when the festival idea emerged. There was no indoor swimming pool on the Island and there was a campaign to raise money for one and the idea of a festival came up. Unfortunately, the fundraiser, the Swimming Pool Association, started getting a lot of publicity which they didn't like and they cut us loose but allowed us to retain the £750 investment they put in, which we paid back after the event. We were introduced to the farmer who owned Hell Field, Jimmy Flux. He only wanted £30 for the rental of the 40-acre barley field, which he would harvest the week before the

The Aynsley Dunbar Retaliation at Godshill. Dunbar, on drums, never found real fame but went on to do session work with the likes of Frank Zappa and Rod Stewart, later playing with Whitesnake.

festival. Appropriately, we knew it would be hell and we would be dealing with stubble and soil with sharp bits poking out. It was also a very unsuitable location because it was quite a trek to get there. Once the project got underway, all hell was let loose with ferocious opposition, but the event was just a few weeks away, so there was no time for opponents to gain an injunction.

"Ronnie scoured the NME and it came to light the American 'underground' act, Jefferson Airplane, was playing in Britain that summer and were looking for one more date, so an agreement was made that they would headline for an advance fee of £1,000 (£20,000 in today's money). Second on the bill would be The Crazy World of Arthur Brown and also booked were The Move, Plastic Penny, Pretty Things, Tyrannosaurus Rex, Aynsley Dunbar Retaliation and Fairport Convention, with John Peel as compere. We now had an event, but the £750 wouldn't pay for all the groups. However, we were able to borrow £1,000 from Malcolm Gould, a kind friend from Freshwater Youth Club days. We contacted the Island's police chief, Supt Paddon, who was very friendly but pointed out a blunder in our *County Press* advert which proclaimed there would be beer tents. We hadn't yet obtained a licence to sell alcohol and he warned our application would very likely be turned down as the licensing magistrates were up in arms about the festival. The solution was for a genuine licensed trader to apply for a license on our behalf and it came to light the proprietor of the Ryde Castle Hotel was desperate for

Festival ticket, printed by Ray Foulk's own company, 'Solent Graphics'

Nº 3614 /B

Saturday August 31st

25/-

THE GREAT SOUTH COAST BANKHOLIDAY POP FESTIVITY

Godshill ISLE OF WIGHT

Nº 3614 /B

Grace Slick of headliners, Jefferson Airplane, backstage at Godshill

The Move at Godshill, Carl Wayne, vocals; Trevor Burton, guitar, and Roy Wood in the background.

money. Ronnie paid her a visit and for a fee of around £100, she took on the concession on our behalf.

"Two flatbed trucks from British Road Services made the stage, scaffold poles were rigged together to create an arch, and black plastic sheeting covered the sides and back. Ronnie approached electrician Harry Garood, who had a little shop in Carisbrooke and knew all about electrics for large-scale events. The field was beautifully lit, with the whole arena illuminated by vivid floodlights — Harry did us proud. Southern Vectis, on the other hand, was singularly unhelpful and wouldn't provide buses to the site. It went smoothly enough. It was a bleak event, as I recall. The weather wasn't very warm, the attendance was not as great as we'd hoped, we only had 10,000 or 15,000 people and most of them were probably from the mainland. Facilities were pretty threadbare. The men's toilets were a trench with a bit of fencing in front and the catering was just a few hotdog vans. Concessions for food were let out to Minghellas, which was then undercut by rogue dealers who had somehow got on to the site. Hostile locals cut the telephone cable to the site and they also turned around some of the festival signage, creating difficulties for travellers.

"The Move had horrendous problems. Nine of their speakers blew up, owing to them playing incredibly loudly and the two power sources blew up back-stage — the generators were quite literally in flames, unable to handle the load. The night was saved by Jefferson Airplane's equipment, including their superior speakers, which were used instead. As one half of Tyrannosaurus Rex, Marc Bolan delivered his quavering lyrics and to illustrate Fire, Arthur Brown donned something like a pie dish, strapped to his head and on fire. Jefferson Airplane began their show at around 2am and were followed by the remaining bands. I remember Jefferson Airplane's light show, the amazing circles of colour whizzing around. On the evening after the festival, there was a party at Yarmouth Youth Club to celebrate its successful execution. The £750 stake from the Swimming Pool Association was paid back but in the days that followed it transpired the festival had lost money — between £500 and £1,000. It was a huge loss by today's standards. No money at all came in from London ticketing outlets, including the Beatles' Apple boutique. As for the ticket agencies, they never passed on the monies from ticket sales. It was a complete rip off. Without these defaults, the festival would have made a good profit. However, we were decided upon another festival the next year — and this time we were set to do it properly."

SOUTH COAST POP FESTIVAL

The organisers of the above event, held at Hell Field, Ford Farm, Godshill, Saturday August 31st, wish to extend their thanks to all who helped to make this event successful. Our special thanks are given to Mr. J. Flux, farmer, Ford Farm; Chief Superintendent Paddon, I.o.W. Constabulary; St. John Ambulance Brigade. It is our hope that next year's event will be even more successful than this year.

RON FOULK, Organiser.

This thanks and acknowledgement notice appeared in the following week's *County Press.*

This elaborate advert appeared acoss a whole page of the *County Press* in the issue preceding the festival. The 'Stop Press' was wildly optimistic, not to say plain misleading. The Beatles, needless to say, did not attend.

holiday Pop Festivity

(NEXT SATURDAY NIGHT)

urday Aug. 31st 6pm to 10 am Next Morning

omplete Festival will be compered by JOHN PEEL, 1 D.J. We regret to announce that due to unforecircumstances Jimmy Savile will not be able to open stival. However, we are pleased to announce that ve added to the bill the latest Beatles ' managed group called " Smile "

SAL "LIGHT SOUND ENVIRONMENT BY ROYAL EGE OF ART. will be arranged from all parts of the Island and there be transport home at various times throughout the night yone not wishing to stay till the end.

OTEL RYDE CASTLE and THE SEAGULL BALLROOM have CELLED THEIR DANCES on AUGUST 31st and will be ing with the catering at the FESTIVAL to support the S.P.A.

TICKETS 25/-

(Limited number available to Island residents in advance only at 20/-) — Buy Now.   From:

ISLE OF WIGHT
INDOOR SWIMMING POOL ASSOCIATION,
177 High Street , Ryde , St. Thomas's Square, Newport.
Also Teagues, Ryde and Newport; Youngs, Cowes, Sandown and Shanklin; John Menzies, Ventnor; George T.V Service, 2 Albert Street, Ventnor; Holdings, Yarmouth, Photo-Wight Freshwater; Lady Katie Boutique, 7 Union Street, Ryde Beardsalls, 53 Regent Street, Shanklin; H. W. Bartlett & Son Bembridge; R. H. Godsland, Trinity Road, East Cowes.

Also at HOTEL RYDE CASTLE and THE SEAGULL BALLROOM RYDE.

HE GREATEST POP FESTIVAL EVER TO BE HELD IN THIS COUNTRY"

ESTIVAL

It has just been confirmed by the Beatles' " Apple " head quarters that John Lennon, Paul McCartney and George Harrison will be at the Festival especially to see the Jefferson Airplane and to promote their new group " SMILE." Other famous celebrities to be announced next week.

SAD END FOR ISLAND DOCTOR

by Brian Greening

Island lifeboat men of old quite rightly hold a special place in our admiration for their many brave adventures years ago. They took to sea in rowing boats, always in the foulest of weather, to go to the aid of unknown sailors whose ships were wrecked or stranded around our Island's coastline, their efforts often straining themselves to the limits of their endurance. Just one example was when the Sirenia was wrecked off Atherfield in 1888.

The first ship to arrive on the scene was a pilot cutter that sailed all around the stricken ship and offered to take off the crew but the Sirenia's captain declined the offer hoping that in time he would be able to re-float his boat.

The Sirenia, en route from San Francisco to Dunkirk, ran onto Atherfield Ledge in March, 1888 with 26 aboard. Two were lost, along with Moses Munt and Tom Cotton, local lifeboatmen.

Meanwhile the lifeboat 'Worcester Cadet' was launched, with her captain Moses Munt and his crew. Having taken off thirteen of the crew, the lifeboat was suddenly turned over and all twenty-six on board were thrown into the sea and although twenty two managed to be got back on board, four were drowned. These were two of the Sirenia's crew and lifeboatmen Moses Munt and Tom Cotton. Both men are buried in the village churchyard. A fuller account of this epic story can be read in Fred Mew's splendid book, 'Back of the Wight.'

However, there was another occasion when the man who sacrificed his life was not a lifeboat man, but simply a Newport doctor, doing what he considered to be his duty. John Wavell was a well-respected Newport man who was aged sixty years old when he died in 1827. He was a member of the local council and had been Mayor of Yarmouth the previous year. He was married with four grown up sons and three daughters. It was in October of that year that his daughter had got married in St. Thomas Church and he was sitting at home alone, his wife having gone to Cheltenham to meet her new son-in-laws family. Possibly he was beside his warm fire drinking a glass of port when he suddenly received a message that a lady on board a boat off Yarmouth was having a miscarriage and was in need of urgent medical attention.

What lay in front of him was not a pleasant journey. First, a ten-mile journey over roads little better than cart tracks, and little in the way of lighting. By the time he got there it was around eight o'clock on that dark and windy winter evening and what lay in front of him was even more unpleasant. He hired a boat and was rowed, through very rough seas, by four experienced local seamen, out to a ship that was anchored, taking shelter, in Totland Bay. The name of the ship was the, 'Happy Return,' an inappropriate name for what would turn into a tragic evening. The ship that was from Penzance, was heading for London carrying a cargo of tin. Onboard were a total of eleven persons comprising crew, women passengers and children.

As the doctor was rowed out to the ship, the weather was found to have moderated somewhat and he was able to board her and attend to the sick lady. It was as he was about to leave the ship that a sudden squall built up, accompanied by thunder and lightning, and the ship was driven inshore on rocks, at a point known as Wardens Ledge. The ship was holed and started to sink immediately. Doctor Wavell was still on deck but a sudden large wave carried him overboard and the men waiting in the rowing boat were unable to reach him. They did manage to save the captain but three women and four children who were still taking refuge in their cabin also sadly drowned. The pilot and the four crew had managed to climb into the rigging and were saved later by two men named Callaway who were from Freshwater, and Timothy Bannister and James Andrews from Yarmouth, who rowed out to the stricken craft around midnight. The men by then had been in the rigging for over three hours before they were rescued.

What added to the heartbreak of the doctor's family was that later they were unable to locate his body and they offered a £5 reward to anybody who found it, a sum of money equivalent today to nearly £500. The reward notice, seen opposite, detailed the clothes that he was wearing. They included breeches and top boots, a black coat and a waistcoat, and a drab great coat. Dressed in such heavy clothes it was immediately evident that he would have quickly been taken down below the waves. Thankfully his body was eventually found and his gold watch was found to have stopped at 10.10 pm, recording the time he was swept overboard.

Following an inquest at Yarmouth, the doctor's body was taken to Newport to be placed in a family vault in St. Thomas Church. In the days following the tragedy Yarmouth went into deep mourning. All the ships in the harbour displayed their colours at mourning height, known better today as half-mast. All windows in private houses and shops were closed and the whole town paid their respects. At the funerals of the married women that were drowned, the pall covering their coffins was supported by six of the town's married women, all dressed in black. For the children the twelve pall bearers were dressed all in white.

Later it was reported that the ship had been partially raised and her cargo of tin, worth in today's currency around half a million pounds, had been salvaged. This was due mainly to a special lifting screw that had been designed and made by the village blacksmith at Winford. This piece of equipment had enabled the ship to be jacked up off the rocks, a no doubt wonderfully inventive design by a man who knew his trade.

In October 1836, The Clarendon, with a cargo of sugar, molasses and rum, was driven ashore at Blackgang and reduced to matchwood in minutes. Onboard were 11 passengers and 17 crew; all but three were drowned. Eighteen of the dead are buried in Chale churchyard.

AND NOW FOR SOMETHING COMPLETELY DIFFERENT

by Alan Stroud

Whenever there were empty spaces to fill in the *County Press* 100 years ago there were always plenty of quirky articles to fill them. Appearing under titles such as '*The Week's News*' or '*Town and County Notes,*' the articles ranged from the sublime to the ridiculous. Without exception, the following articles are all genuine.

In September 1889, a new word was invented when David Dunford, a carriage driver of West Cowes, was summoned for assaulting George Millwood, another carriage driver. As the *County Press* put it, "Millwood stated that he was on the Parade when Dunford drove up and struck him in the face. Dunford said Millwood provoked him by calling out to him. His young blood could not stand it and he gave him a clout. He said Millwood was the 'insultingest' man in Cowes. – Fined 5 shillings with 11 shillings costs."

Cowes Parade and Pier, a scene that would have been very familiar to the "insultingest man in Cowes"

From the insultingest man in Cowes to a sarcasticatious one. In January 1891, someone signing himself 'a resident' wrote to the letters column of the *County Press* : "Sir, – I see in the paper that there are prosecutions for selling adulterated milk. I hope such powers may be exercised in West Cowes, as for some time past the water we are supplied with is so white, and the milk so blue, that on dark mornings it is nearly impossible to distinguish one from the other, Yours, a resident."

And some days it just doesn't pay to get out of bed. From May 1891 comes this sorry tale : "At J. Samuel White's shipyard at Cowes on Friday, a young gentleman named Cunningham was using a circular saw when one of his hands came into contact with it, the thumb being nearly severed. Unfortunately, he then put his other hand on the top of the injured one and the thumb of that hand was also nearly severed."

Most of us don't want to be shot from a cannon or eat light bulbs. By and large, we're happy to pay to watch someone else do it for us. Unfortunately for the 'someone else' involved, it's going to end in tears sometimes, as it did in April 1894 : "An inquest was held at London on the body of Owen Williams, 42, who earned money by frequenting public houses and swallowing bottles, saucers and other things. Evidence was given that he died from internal obstruction. A post-mortem revealed inside Mr. Williams numerous pieces of cork and tin foil, a lead bullet, a piece of string with corks attached, eight bronze pennies, pipe stems and a piece of leather nine inches long with a hook at each end."

Maybe Mr Williams was as mad as a hatter. But then again - perhaps not, for in 1900, *County Press* readers were informed : "Though the phrase 'as mad as a hatter' is a household one, it does not appear to be altogether true, for according to the annual report of the London County Council Asylum Committee there were only four mad hatters in London last year."

And what went on here in 1904, we shall never know; perhaps it's for the best : "Miss Charmley, of Accrington, was found gagged and bound in a coal cellar, with a note reading 'Revenge is sweet' pinned on her dress."

The same probably applies to this tale from 1906 : "A sailor dressed as a fashionable lady badly beat three constables who tried to arrest him at Croydon on Tuesday."

Upper High Street, Ryde, in the 1890s.

Newport High Street in the 1880s. The man is outside Padlock House, an ironmongers shop. Their trademark, a giant padlock can just be seen at the top of the picture.

Back on the Island, in 1908 goings-on at East Cowes were raising eyebrows : "Correction - In order to avoid creating any wrong impression we are asked to state that there was no dancing at the East Cowes Congregational tennis social reported last week." Heaven forbid.

Meanwhile, in 1909 William Gauntlett, described as a butler, was "charged with making obscene drawings in the public convenience in Watchbell-lane. In consequence of complaints P.C. Collins was instructed to watch the convenience and he saw defendant making the drawings with a piece of pencil on the previous day. When the prisoner left he followed and arrested him. Pieces of pencil and chalk were found upon him. Fined 15s. and costs."

Still with toilets, in a public lavatory at Ryde in 1910, "Charles Atrill was summoned for the use of profane language at Ryde Esplanade toilets. – John Rogers, lavatory attendant, told the Court that defendant's conduct was most disgusting, and when remonstrated with, he asked 'What the —— he had to do with it,' adding, 'I help to pay for the —— place' and witness 'was —— well paid to clean it'. Fined 10s. and 10s.6d. costs."

Well, serves him —— ing right.

by Brian Greening

A few years ago I came across a letter in the *County Press* sent in by a reader recalling the Newport that he knew as a boy, that was a time around 1824. It made fascinating reading and described a Newport that quite naturally bears no resemblance to the town we know today. At each point of the compass as the town extended into its surroundings very little building had taken place. From the top of the town there were no houses either side of the Mall and a clear uninterrupted view of Parkhurst Forest was to be seen by looking north. Beyond Medina Avenue the only dwellings there were were the terrace of ten Oyster Shell cottages, the large house at Mount Pleasant owned by the Kirkpatrick banking family, and Shide dairy. At Fairlee and Hunnyhill a similar scene existed. There were no houses at Hunnyhill until one reached the barracks at Parkhurst and the Workhouse, and exiting the town from Coppins Bridge, just a couple of cottages and the large Fairlee House was all there was to be seen. The article left a wonderful picture of the open panorama that existed at the time and I recently, rather pompously, thought that I might do a similar thing by recalling the Coppins Bridge area that I knew in 1950. Maybe in a hundred years time others might find it educational.

In this photo from the early 1950s three shops can be clearly seen, with the, by then empty, 'Coopers' Arms' public house to the fore on the right.

I lived near the cemetery in Fairlee Road and my walk to the Infant School involved walking as far as the Police Station, then across the road and up Staplers. In those days, just past Broadlands House was a large rookery and high on a bank were old Nissen huts used by Canadian soldiers who were billeted in the area during the war. Many of these young men went off to fight at Dieppe, a forerunner of D-Day, and would have lost their lives.

I enjoyed school but hated the prayer we were made to recite each day before going home. It went, "If I should die before I wake, I pray the Lord my soul to take." That, I was not happy with. The teacher never knew how close I came to departing this earth at that time as whilst still there I was knocked down by an Army lorry and spent four days in Ryde Hospital.

My progress to the senior boy's school in Barton Road meant a slight detour, Staplers being avoided, so I took a walk down to Coppins Bridge and then a gentle walk up Barton Road. On the way I passed the several establishments that were there, now etched deep in my memory. First was 'Hunter and Coombes', a ships chandlers, then Vic Clark's hairdressers shop in what had previously been the Victoria Inn. It was directly opposite the, by then empty, Coopers Arms pub, these two ale houses being separated by Gasworks Cut, a rough path leading down and through to the quay, via a path beneath the railway viaduct we knew as the Arches. Three shops then came together, Albie Fry's greengrocery shop, Mrs. Snow's fish and chip shop and then Mr. Palmer's sweet shop with all the goods displayed in the shop window where a cat could often be seen sunning itself. Then high above me was the large metal railway bridge over which trains went to and fro to Sandown. The last piece of architecture was a large hoarding that each week advertised the films being shown at the local cinemas. We young lads would stand there to see whether it had a 'U' certificate or an 'A', the latter meaning we had to be accompanied by an adult to gain admittance.

My school class of 1953. I can still name all but three but do not, however, ask me what I had for breakfast.

Coppins Bridge to me was the centre of my universe. I would often see Mr. Jack Powell who became the first Labour Mayor of Newport. Most mornings when I saw him, however, he was on his way home to his house in Highfield Road, from shift work on the railways, leaning over the wall, gazing down into the river and smoking a Woodbine. Very often one of his sons, Raymond, would be hurrying the other way pushing an old pram, on his way to the gasworks to get a sack of coke, it being cheaper if you collected it yourself.

The real centre piece of the area was, however, the metal railway bridge that went high across the road taking trains out of and into Newport. It might be an engine pulling trucks full of chalk from the pit at Shide over the bridge on the way to the cement works at Dodnor. Then of course there were the passenger trains, belching steam, taking folk across the Island, linking Cowes and Sandown. It was this train that brought one of our teachers, Papa Warder, each day from his home at Sandown and returned him each evening. One day, two boys who had felt Papa's cane during the day were beneath the bridge as he went back to Sandown. They waved to him, but only used two fingers. The next morning they had another caning on each hand. Reading these words may mean little to many but hopefully one day they will educate those that follow behind us. So I think I have made it clear, despite a sweet shop and a fish and chip shop my favourite was that old iron railway bridge that leaves me with happier memories than that large, always congested roundabout that we have today. When they did away with the railways why didn't they build a flyover that could have followed the line of the railway? If you do ever get an answer it will have the words "health and safety" in it.

Coppins railway bridge. The Grand Cinema hoarding is for the Peter Sellers film 'Two Way Stretch' released in January 1960.

Coppins railway bridge and Snooks Hill in a 1924 aerial photograph.

"Perhaps The Most Beautiful Drive In The Island"

by Alan Stroud

The Island's geology is no respecter of peoples' property – ask Island Roads and the residents of St Lawrence Undercliff. Landslips, major and minor, have been unceremoniously dumping Islanders' homes and possessions into the sea for thousands of years. The coastline from Compton right round to Yaverland is a geological nightmare and is and always will be, forever on the move. And it can disappear at a fairly alarming pace at times. Since the first ordnance survey map was drawn in 1810, the cliff edge at Blackgang has moved nearly 300 metres inland and in 1799, the whole of nearby Pitlands Farm, over 100 acres, slipped into the sea and disappeared beneath the waves.

The coach is stopped alongside 'Chad Rock,' a local landmark until both it and the road were swept away in the 1928 landslip

The next big fall was in July 1928. It had been expected as the signs had been there for all to see for several months. Deep cracks had appeared in the clifftop fields at Blackgang and lower down the cliffs wide fissures had opened in the clay soil. It was obvious that the land was on the move and it prompted the Council to close the undercliff road linking Chale to Ventnor. It was a good job they did. Within days, 100,000 tons of rock had tumbled down, completely burying the road, seen above. Nature having given notice of the event, the man from the *County Press* was actually there when it happened, "The cliff crumbled and thundered down to the road below. Clouds of dust arose blotting out the view. In a minute it was all over, leaving the changed cliff line, a vanished road, a handful of half-dazed people, and a dead rabbit,"

Two months later, a massive landslide finished the job and carried the entire road away, the *County Press* reporting, "An area of at least 50 acres is literally moving seawards at a truly alarming pace. Since Wednesday,

The Blackgang to Ventnor Road seen just before, and during the 1928 landslip.

the land has been moving so rapidly as to change the whole face of the landscape every few hours. Fifty feet of the roadway cracked and slipped away, the surface of the road turning inwards and downwards in the most astounding fashion as it went … The whole area was scoured with cracks, which by Thursday had become huge fissures 20 feet wide. Several acres of land had sunk to a depth of from 20 to 30 feet in places."

And that was that. It was the end of the road described at the time by the *County Press* as, "perhaps the most popular and beautiful drive in the Island." Today, the two stranded ends can still be seen; one just past the entrance to Blackgang Chine, while the other end has become the car park at Knowles Farm viewpoint.

After the landslip.

By the early seventies there were only three occupied houses in the landslip area; Southview, which had become a holiday centre for naturists; Sandrock Spring House and across the road, Sandrock Cottage, both owned by the Young family of 'Young's TV and Radio' shops.

In 1978, they all fell victim to another massive landslip. Richard Young was interviewed the following year by Henry Hislop for his programme on Isle of Wight Hospital Radio and told him of the night he lost his house. And chilling reading it is... "Sandrock Spring House really was a super house; built like a Swiss chalet, with superb views across the sea and lovely grounds around it. We lived there for 34 years. Across the road we had Sandrock Spring Cottage which in itself was a very charming place."

"It was March 1978 when the terrible things happened. The first warning I had was when Chris, my son, called me in the shop at Ryde and said he'd heard tree roots cracking, which alarmed him, and he said, 'Dad, I think you should come back.' I came as quick as I could but it wasn't quick enough. As I went to walk down to the house I met my wife and Chris, who'd already told her, 'We've got to get out now.' As they came out, the kitchen floor was beginning to rise up where the house was compressing with the movement of the large mass of earth. There was almost a quarter of a mile of ground on the move; it wasn't just a little tiny bit."

"We stood and watched all the electric light poles come over. It was terrible. They were flashing and banging away. I came back to the house the next morning hoping it might have stood it, but it wasn't to be. It was still intact - the roof was quite good as a matter of fact - but it was cracked very, very badly. Doors were lopsided - it was a job to open them - and the poor old cottage across the road was just a heap of rubble with the roof laying

Sandrock Spring Cottage after the 1978 landslip.

on the top like a hat. Everything in the house was topsy-turvy. The beautiful antique staircase in the house had all gone crooked - you had a job to walk up it. Most of the stuff in the cottage got wrecked. It was very beautiful. It was a gift to have been permitted to live in such a place. It all blended in so beautifully with the surroundings. It was fantastic. Even now I go down there once or twice a week but, of course, there's no house any more."

The landslips continue to this day, the attractions at Blackgang Chine bearing witness to that. To add insult to injury, the owners of the attraction, the Dabell family, lost Gore Cliff Cottage in 1994.

The most recent slip of any size was in 2003. It certainly won't be the last.

MUST I REALLY TAKE THAT, DOCTOR?

by Brian Greening

The study of medicine has come a long way in recent years, although stark similarities are developing with how it was practised more than 60 years ago. It was in 1952 that *County Press* cartoonist Tom Smitch made his acerbic observation of GP surgery waiting times, at a time when the development of drugs and treatment techniques was changing apace. We have moved on from the medieval practice of blood letting and the use of leeches to remove bad blood, and that of giving women horse's saliva to restore lust. Thankfully too, the old cough cure practice of collecting snails, removing their shells and placing them in a porous bag with half a pound of sugar and collecting the juice has long ceased. The ancient hot iron cure for haemorrhoids will not be explored. In 1775, yet another cure for the common cold was published. Sudden changes of the weather during the winter months brought forth coughs and colds that were, it was said, seldom dangerous and easily cured by avoiding solid meats and living sparingly. Frequently sipping warm broth, water gruel, weak rum or a gin toddy, and staying indoors as much as possible, especially mornings and evenings, was recommended. If, however, business compelled going outdoors, the prudent should be well-clothed. At night, on retiring, a basin of sack whey with 20-30 drops of spirits of harts' horn was recommended. According to the advice of the celebrated Dr Cheney, it was more to be depended upon than any balsamic or pectoral medicines. If the cough was troublesome, a teaspoonful of sugar candy and spermaceti, or linseed oil taken several times a day would give certain relief. Malt liquors, especially those that were strong, should be avoided and the body, if constipated, could be kept open by a dose of Dafly's Elixir or Glauber's salts. If there was an appearance of fever, five to six grains of Doctor James's powder, taken at bedtime and repeated if necessary, would be found effectual.

I have an old book written much later, around 1870, entitled "Till the Doctor Comes." It gave advice to Victorians on the treatment to be followed for various ailments. Foremost in these were suggestions on treating scalds and burns, common in those days of open ranges and unprotected coal fires.

13

THE SICK ROOM.

IF you are so fortunate as to have a choice of rooms, do not put your patient into one which is dark and gloomy, but let it be light and cheerful, and with a fireplace if possible.

If the illness be fever, something wrong with the eyes or brain, or other sickness requiring quiet, a back room away from the family will answer best; the patient will not care to look at anything or to speak much, and quietness is necessary. But if he be suffering from an accident, let him be near the rest of the family where you can speak to him. This will help to keep him contented and cheerful, for it will be an amusement to him to watch your movements while you are going on with your work, and it will save time in waiting upon him.

Do not fix upon a room near a cesspool or a pigsty, or other bad-smelling place. A pig is a capital thing for a cottager to have. It gives him something to look after, and it saves many scraps from being wasted. A flitch or two of good bacon is excellent furniture in a house-place, but however useful our curly-tailed friend may be in his proper place, he is not a nice neighbour for a sick room.

67

POISONS AND POISONING.

SO many substances of a poisonous nature being used in manufactures, amongst farmers, and also in private houses, it will be useful to have a guide to refer to in case of accident; for in almost every case of poisoning the remedy must be given immediately, or we cannot expect to succeed. I give here the names in common use, and under one head I include various articles made from the same substance. For instance, to the word mercury you will find calomel, corrosive sublimate, white precipitate, vermilion, which are all mercury, but in different forms.

Arsenic : Scheele's green, ague drops, rat poison, etc.—*Symptoms :* Pain and burning heat of stomach, dryness of throat, cramps, purging, vomiting. — *Treatment :* Give large quantities of milk and raw eggs, lime-water or flour-and-water. Then castor oil.

Artimony : Butter of antimony, tartar emetic, etc. — *Symptoms :* Severe vomiting, cramps, faintness, purging. — *Treatment :* Plenty of strong tea. If you have no common tea at hand, use an infusion of oak, elm, sloe, currant, or blackberry bark and leaves. Or

Two typical pages of advice from the book, dated around 1885, with the cover shown on opposite page.

Those suffering from fever, or eye or brain disorders, were recommended a quiet location, possibly a room to the rear of the house. However, it was stated this room should not be near a cesspool or a pigsty. It lauded the value of our curly-tailed friend to the cottager but he was not a nice neighbour for the sick room. Floors were to be clean boarded and kept sweet by scrubbing and elbow grease, carpets not being recommended. Chimneys should be kept clear to avoid smoke blowing back into the room. A hair mattress was recommended but it was

recognised cost could be prohibitive, so as an alternative, good clean chaff was suggested as mattress filler. The book went on to say it was a mistake to assume nursing was solely women's work, for the extra strength possessed by a man was often beneficial. There were said to be five qualifications required by a nurse, namely: "Sobriety, cleanliness, firmness, gentleness and patience." The contents of the medicine chest were next discussed and it was suggested this should always be kept locked. It should include rolls of old linen, calico and flannel, all torn into strips, plus a little lint and sticking plaster, a pair of scissors, some pins, and a few large needles that should be ready threaded. Liquids should include castor oil, Friar's Balsam, turpentine, senna leaves, Epsom salts, a small bottle of laudanum – marked poison, of course — and a pint bottle of linseed oil and lime water.

The author advised against keeping simple ointment, because it did not keep well, but suggested a little clean lard was to be obtained at the time if needed. A jug showing measures of teaspoonfuls on one side and tablespoons on the other was also suggested, and lastly a feeding cup, as many patients should not be raised, simply kept lying flat. Should a feeding cup not be available, then a teapot with a small spout was suggested. All no doubt good advice at a time when doctors charged a fee for visiting the sick.

Two complaints of years ago, namely the painful whitlows and stomach worms are also discussed but sadly space is not available to elaborate on them. I recall my father, who was a gardener for most of his life, suffering mainly from two ailments — chapped hands and a heavy cold, both attributed to outdoor working. The chapped hands I know he found extremely painful and whenever he had a heavy cold he would boil up a couple of large onions that he would place in a bowl and begin by inhaling the vapour given off, while having a towel over his head. He would then proceed to eat the onions. The only effect, I believe, was that they made him perspire during the night. This sweating was another Victorian suggestion but their advice of visiting a Turkish bath was not much use to my father on the Isle of Wight. He worked hard for all his life but was sadly afflicted with Parkinson's disease about a month after retirement. Today, a cure for this and many other aliments still has to be found but when they do, no doubt another disease will come along and confuse the doctors for another 100 years. Such is life and death.

An early 1950s cartoon by *County Press* cartoonist, Tom Smitch, that could really have been penned yesterday. It appears that seeing a doctor today takes equally as long today as it did seventy years ago.

The Most Daring And Extensive Robbery Newport Has Ever Known

by Alan Stroud

It is a quiet afternoon in Newport in late March, 1896. On the corner of Nodehill and Chapel Street, roughly where Bernard's shoe shop is today, stands the shop of elderly batchelor Mr Pike. He is a gold and silver dealer, and his stock is worth several thousand pounds. Sometime after 1 o'clock he leaves the shop for twenty minutes to take lunch in his living quarters at the back of the shop. Later, he was to claim that he had definitely locked the shop door before leaving. Perhaps he had. Or perhaps he hadn't. Whichever it was, it was the costliest lunch break Newport had ever seen, for on his return he was alarmed to find that someone had been in the shop.

Looking around, he immediately noticed to his horror that a tray full of guineas and half-guineas was missing from the window. Panic-stricken, he rushed to his safe, which he later agreed he had left unlocked, and there his worst fears were confirmed. A large cash-box was missing. It contained £1200 in gold sovereigns, £20 in silver, six Jubilee £5 pieces, four Jubilee £2 pieces, a gold watch and gold and silver Army medals. The total loss came to £1500. The County Press reported, "Mr. Pike, who is sole occupier of the premises, and rather feeble with the weight of 76 years pressing upon him, at once communicated his alarming discovery to his neighbour, George Chiverton who promptly summoned the police. Div. Sergeant. Adams and Sergeant. T. Cass were soon on the scene to commence their investigations."

EXTRAORDINARY ROBBERY AT NEWPORT.

A SILVER DEALER'S UNDESIRABLE CUSTOMER.

£1200 AND COSTLY COINS AND MEDALS STOLEN IN BROAD DAYLIGHT.

AN IMPORTANT CLUE OBTAINED.

On Wednesday afternoon last, considerable consternation was created in Newport by the report that an extraordinarily daring and extensive shop theft had just been perpetrated at the premises of Mr John Pike, dealer in old silver &c., in Upper St James's-street. About 2.15 on the afternoon in question Mr Pike, on re-entering his shop after temporary absence in the living apartments of his premises, was almost dumbfounded at discovering that in the very short interval a thief or thieves had affected an entrance by picking the lock of the shop door, and had got clean away with current coin of the realm, a large number of rare and valuable old coins, war medals, and other property, to the total value of over £1500. Mr Pike who is sole occupier of the premises and rather feeble with the weight of 74 years pressing upon him, at once communicated his startling discovery to his neighbour, Mr George Chiverton, who promptly summoned the police. Div. Sgt Adams and Sgt T Cass were soon on the scene to commence the investigations and a constable or two posted in the vicinity moved up and down the numbers of people who were speedily

How the *County Press* reported the robbery.

Mr Pike's shop, set back on the corner of Nodehill and Chapel Street. Bernard's shoe shop now occupies the site of Mr Pike's front garden.

According to a later *County Press* report, Mr Pike was "a bachelor, who had lived alone in rigidly modest style, though possessed of a considerable fortune obtained by close attention to business; a fortune which, with an aversion to banking, he seems to have hoarded at home."

£1,500 was a huge sum for those days. It is difficult to put a modern-day value on his loss, but for each of the policemen investigating the case £1,500 would have represented over 20 year's wages. Mr. Pike claimed the lock of the shop door had been picked but rather pointedly, the *County Press* commented, "How the door could have been picked in broad daylight without detection by passers-by, seems passing strange." Passing strange indeed.

It transpired that a man carrying a heavy, black bag had been seen to leave the shop and hurry down South Street, "presumably to catch the 3-o'clock train." This man, supposedly "a well-known convicted thief" was now the prime suspect but alas, he had vanished. Nearly three months then passed with no signs of an arrest. Mr Pike's hopes, like his money, had all but gone until late June when he finally got some good news. The suspect, a Charles Johnson, had been arrested in London.

The problem was that far from living a life of luxury, all the signs were that Johnson was as poor as a church mouse. He was found living in 'poor and squalid' lodgings in the East End of London and there was no sign at all of Mr Pike's money at the scene. In fact, Johnson appeared to be as penniless as Mr Pike now was.

Official and other Notices

THE LATE ROBBERY AT NEWPORT

PUBLIC NOTICE

IT having come to the knowledge of the undersigned that certain false and wicked slanders are in circulation respecting him, this is to give PUBLIC NOTICE that proceedings will be taken against any person or persons who shall hereafter repeat such slanders; and a REWARD of FIVE POUNDS is hereby offered to any individual whose evidence shall obtain the conviction in a Court of Justice of such person or persons.   GEORGE CHIVERTON

89, St. James's-street, Newport, IW, May 9, 1896.

The Newport rumour mill forced Mr Pike's neighbour into placing a notice in the *County Press*.

"I was standing at my shop door, where I spend pretty near half of my life." Mr Ledicott's shop on the corner of Crocker and Holyrood Street.

Newport High Street as Mr. Pike would have known it in the 1890s.

Nonetheless, he was arrested and brought to the Island by a Scotland Yard detective, to be charged with robbery. Described as "a young man of good appearance," the evidence against him was flimsy at best. He had just two shillings on him when he was found and not unreasonably told the arresting detective, "You have made a mistake. If I stole £1500, do you think I would have sold a rug for five shillings this morning?" Johnson then took the detective to a nearby pawnbroker's shop where it was confirmed that he had indeed pawned a rug that morning; not only that, the previous week he had also pawned a gold ring for eight shillings. It was hardly the mark of a man supposed to have over £1500 to his name.

In court Mr Pike was called, the *County Press* reporting, "Witness, feeble with age and apparently still considerably worried over his loss, when asked if he remembered the afternoon of 25th March last, answered pathetically, I do, to my sorrow. Mr Mould (prosecuting) Q. He took the cash box and the gold too? A. Yes, he took it all, sir (*a laugh*). Q. Have you got it back? A. No, sir; I wish I had (*laughter*)."

In a blow to the prosecution, all the witnesses, apart from one, agreed that Johnson was not the man they had seen struggling with a weighty bag that afternoon, the landlord of the Railway Medina telling the court quite firmly, "That is not the man" (*applause*). Another, equally sure, was William Ledicott, owner of the Old Curiosity Shop in Holyrood Street, "I was standing at my shop door, where I spend pretty near half of my life (*laughter*) at about 2.30, when I noticed a man carrying a very heavy bag towards the station. It struck me that he had something more than feathers in his bag (*laughter, in which prisoner joined*). Prisoner was not that man, I am perfectly prepared to swear."

Despite the lack of evidence, Johnson was committed for trial at Winchester in October where to no one's great surprise he was acquitted. Poor Mr Pike was described as "too ill to attend Court.

Sadly, Mr Pike would never see his money again. Just six weeks later he was found dead in the shop, in the very same room he had been born in. His death went unrecorded in the 'Deaths' column since there was no family to place it there for him but it was marked in the 'Newport' column of November 28, 1896, the *County Press* reporting, "He died from apoplectic seizure and senile decay at the age of 76. To one of his disposition, the recent loss of over £1500 was a great shock, and though his fortune was by no means exhausted, the loss evidently told upon him in his declining days."

by Brian Greening

I recently discovered some old newspaper cuttings of the exploits of Newport's football team in the 1950s. It was a time when I wore short trousers but those cuttings brought back memories of a time when Newport regularly progressed through several rounds of the FA Cup and often brought league opposition to their ground at Church Litten. On match days there was a steady stream of supporters going along Town Lane to be met by a man selling a match day programme that cost 2d. I recall the days when Andover visited the ground because they had a footballer by the name of McCarthy, a tricky and speedy winger who was always a problem for the Newport defence. What was unusual for those days was that he was a black man.

You paid to enter the Church Litten ground at a tiny kiosk and then had a decision to make, go to the left and stand behind the goal that fronted the cattle market, or go to the right and stand on the bank that separated the ground from Gould, Hibberd and Randall's mineral water factory. All the players were my heroes, be it Alan Brown, a diminutive full-back who would resort to amputation at the hip to stop his winger, to Paddy O'Connor, another tiny man who could have written a book on the art of diving to gain a penalty, while Johnny Mitchell was a skilful

NEWPORT 1952/3
BACK : FRED COOKE, P. TAULBUT, H. LEGGE, R. SLADE, A. KNIGHT.
FRONT : F. GRIST, A. BROWN, P. O'CONNOR, J.ANDERSON, D.BRYANT, J. MITCHELL, R. GILLFILLAN

winger. Roy Gillfillan was the ace goal scorer and the team was captained by ex-Portsmouth professional Jock Anderson. One of the nicest men I ever met while playing football was Newport's centre-half Peter Taulbut, a true gentleman and a majestic centre half who would help opponents to their feet with a smile after slowing their progress toward goal. Later, in my late teens, I had the pleasure of playing with Peter when he ended his career playing for Sandown.

Reverting to those newspaper cuttings, I was reminded of the tremendous crowds Newport used to attract. Grown men would turn up wearing their yellow and blue scarves with a few of the more passionate supporters carrying bells or those old fashioned klaxon-sounding rattles. One game I recall was when Newport were drawn

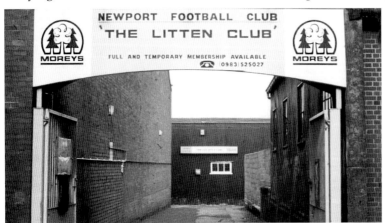

The entrance to the former Church Litten football ground.

at home in the first round proper of the FA Cup against Watford in 1956. This was the fourth time in five years the club had progressed thus far in that historic competition, having previously been drawn away twice to Swindon. A spokesman for the club stated they expected a crowd of more than 8,000 to turn up. The Watford team, not wishing to travel on the day of the match, stayed the Friday night at a Ryde hotel. Watford won the match 6-0. The two games of the season were on Boxing Day and Good Friday, when Cowes and Newport met in a local derby. Feelings ran high both on and off the pitch and it was rare for either team to end with eleven players, those going off being either injured or sent off by the referee. Remember, there were no substitutes in those days.

Local football matches attracted huge crowds, especially when teams such as Seaview, Brading, West Wight and Parkhurst were involved. Spectators would travel across the Island to see such players as Len Beaumont, Nobby Scovell, John Southcott, Maurice Price, Tony Grimwade, and Arnold Olive play in a match, the two latter lads being known to score over one hundred goals in a season.

With the football season over, I took to going to Seaclose to watch Fairlee Cricket Club play their matches. I recall all their players even today. Opening batsman Joe Dark, school teacher, Bill Milton, Les and Fred Hall,

Freddie Sims, the amazing Roy Pridmore, John Reagan, and wicket keeper, Harry Canning. Their fast bowlers were John Brookes and Roger Farrington. My task was to stand on the scoreboard and put up the total runs scored or the number of wickets that had fallen. Umpire for Fairlee was Wally Moore, the club's secretary, a man of few words but a polite and gentle man and a true lover of the game.

Newport supporters at an unknown away match in the 1950s. Charging to the front ringing his bell is 'Nobber' Knowles.

Sunday mornings were taken up either playing cricket or football at Seaclose. There was never a Sunday football league in those days as the local council refused to sanction such a thing. At either game, up to 40 men turned up. Football teams would be picked around 11am, often numbering close to 20 players a side and the game would continue until 1pm. There was never a referee but disputes were minimal. One player I recall was George Willett, who would leave a pair of boots in a hole in the riverbank and was often seen emptying water from them before he put them on. The cricket matches were fast-paced affairs with just one batsman facing up to eight bowlers who came at him alternately at a rate of knots. Names are recalled such as Ron Ash, a doughty left hander, Vic Deacon, Sid Hunt, Vic Hayles, Ben 'Banjo' Whitewood and diminutive Denny Houghton. Disputes were few and once you were out, another batsman took your place and before the morning was over you could guarantee at least three innings and several spells of bowling.

Although many might disagree, standards have diminished and no longer do crowds of well over two thousand turn up to watch a local football game. Apathy and money have taken charge and Newport will soon be playing their home games nearer Whippingham than Newport. Ryde no longer have a team or a ground. One thing they cannot take from me are my memories of those stalwarts of the past. Bullet head Harry Legg heading clear a heavy, wet, leather football, that wizard of the dribble Roy Gilfillan, and gentleman Peter Taulbut. Who, I wonder, will today's generation talk of with such affection in fifty years time?

Vast crowds watching a 1950s FA cup match at Church Litten football ground.

THE DAY GURNARD WAS BOMBED - BRENDA WAS THERE

by Alan Stroud

Imagine a sunny summer's day at Gurnard beach, just down from the Woodvale Hotel, with laughing children swimming and splashing in the waves as their mothers look on. Now imagine a German fighter plane appearing in the sky, swooping low to drop a bomb on the terrified mothers and children. Brenda Richards, now in her eighties, doesn't have to imagine it. She was there when it happened.

Brenda is my wife's Aunt and what follows is just part of the fascinating story of her childhood that she has written for her family. Aged seven, Brenda Young, as she then was, lived at 6, Broadfields Avenue at Cowes. One afternoon in the summer of 1941 she went to the beach with her mother ....

"It was a never-to-be-forgotten day. We were in the water swimming when the siren went and enemy planes were heard approaching. Mum called to us and we all ran to the public lavatories on the green. The air raid warden was there and he kept saying 'Keep calm. Keep calm.' The building was crowded with women and

Brenda Richards, nee Young.

children and a woman started screaming. Mum, in her 'sergeant major voice', said, 'Shut up that bloody row!' and there was a deathly hush. No one dared to panic after that! The planes got nearer and the drone of their engines was horrible. Then came the whistle of a bomb, softly at first, then louder and louder until WHOOMPH!, the doors and windows were blown in and we were all pushed as though by a giant hand - there was brick and glass debris everywhere. When the 'all clear' sounded we filed out, clambering over the rubble, to find a huge bomb crater with earth, rocks and stones piled up to where we had been sheltering. Mercifully, no one was hurt and everyone felt we had experienced a miracle. We all knew we could be killed at any time, but right now we were alive and very thankful for that.

"I was six when war was declared and twelve when it ended so most of my formative years were in wartime. I clearly remember my parents in the kitchen one day listening to the radio, looking very solemn. We went in and Mum told us war had been declared. I asked my sister Janet, 'What is a war?' She said, 'You know. Cowboys and Indians and things.'

"We had our windows criss-crossed with sticky tape to stop any bomb blast from shattering glass into the room and everyone had to obey the 'blackout' so we had black blinds across all the windows and doors. Outside it was pitch black.

This is Arctic Road, Cowes, the morning after the huge bombing raid of May 4/5th, 1942 which killed 70 people. Although it was illegal to photograph bomb damage, this picture somehow appeared in a Toronto newspaper six weeks later, captioned 'A Nazi raid did this to a south coast town in England.'

There were no street lamps, and no lights in houses anywhere.

"Air raid shelters were built in the school playground and whenever the siren went we had to walk, not run, to the shelter. Once inside we would listen to stories the teacher read. If the raid was overhead and very noisy we would sing loudly.

"During the Cowes blitz of May 1942 there were bombing raids every night for over a week. One night we were told to leave our house and run to the shelter on the opposite side of the road. It was the most frightening experience of the war as far as I was concerned. An incendiary bomb had fallen on a nearby bungalow and when we opened the back door to go, the light was horrifying and the heat from the raging fires hurt our faces. Huge balls of flame shot up into the

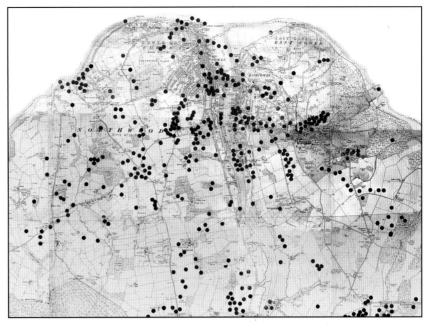

This is part of a map made during the war by the Civil Defence to accurately record the location of every bomb that fell on the Island. The full map, held at the County Records Office, is a patchwork quilt of over 60 maps, each two foot by two foot, the whole map measuring 18 feet by 15 feet.

sky and the noise of the fire and the roaring and crackling was terrible. I clutched the door post screaming, not wanting to go outside. Mum grabbed an old coat and threw it over my head so I couldn't see and we all ran, me being dragged, to the shelter.

The following week the women and children from Broadfields Avenue were taken to the woods at Porchfield. We slept in the back of some lorries. Those precious nights of peace and quiet after the dreadful noise of the bombing are indelibly printed in my mind and are among my most treasured memories. I was seven; old enough to appreciate the sound of the birds, and the wildflowers. It was springtime and we were woken by the dawn chorus and the fresh smell of the woodland. In those woods, and in those circumstances, I discovered my great need of the peacefulness of the countryside and God seemed to be very near in the calm of the darkness.

On VE Day, victory was celebrated and church bells, forbidden during the war, rang out in wonderful celebration. We celebrated! We danced in the streets! We had street parties with lemonade, jam sandwiches and jelly and trifle!

In a way, growing up in war time was a great privilege. Seeing so much sadness and danger and knowing that my schoolfriends who wore black armbands were showing they mourned a loved one, and knowing that at any time we could be killed, made us learn compassion and love. It demonstrated to all of us that we should live for today and get up in the morning and think, Today I shall be happy and live each minute in peace and harmony. God gave us life. We should be thankful and not waste any of it."

(Sadly, Brenda has died since this article first appeared.)

A wartime photograph of Brenda, left, with her younger sister Janet

What do I do...

if my home is made uninhabitable by a bomb?

I ask a warden or a policeman to direct me to the allotted Rest Centre. If I have relatives or friends to whom I can go, I apply to the Public Assistance Authority for a travel voucher. If my home is not completely destroyed, I go to the Town Hall or consult the Local Authority to see if and when temporary repairs can be done. If I have become separated from my family or my children and cannot find them, I ask for help at the nearest Citizens' Advice Bureau or the Police Station. (The Rest Centre or the Police will supply all these addresses.)

Cut this out—and keep it!

Issued by The Ministry of Information
Space presented to the Nation
by the Brewers' Society

A grim list of instructions from 1940 for those unlucky enough to be bombed.

by Brian Greening

One thing those who sat at Westminster reluctantly gave away almost two hundred years ago was the eventual movement toward the right of 'one man, one vote. This procedure commenced in 1832 but it started as a trickle and only extended to around one in eight of the male population (sorry ladies, you would have to wait almost another hundred years). Locally, for Sir Leonard Troughear Holmes, Lord of the Manor of Westover, the procedure prior to his death in 1825 was simply a case of, either putting himself forward or naming a couple of colleagues to become the two Members of Parliament for Newport, no doubt in return for a modest fee. In 1818, he chose a good local man, Charles Duncombe, of Duncombe Hall, York, as his partner and there followed a grand celebratory dinner at the Green Dragon Inn, near where the Conservative Club in Newport is today. In the chair for the evening was the Mayor of Newport, Benjamin Jolliffe, who for the record, did not live within the borough but had a home at Merstone.

Sir Leonard Troughear Holmes

The introduction of mechanisation years ago, such as threshing machines, resulted in many men becoming unemployed and this did little to endear the employees to their employer and these machines were later often vandalised and hayricks burnt down, the punishment for which, if caught, was transportation, or at worst, the gallows. Thankfully we do not see the staff in supermarkets today resorting to such actions over the introduction of the self-scanning machines, that have the same effect in eliminating jobs as those threshing machines did. Thus, when any member of the aristocracy and their supporters came to town seeking votes, they were given a rough reception.

However, your vote after 1832 was not secret and it was easy to discover the way a person voted. In later years, for farm labourer's living in tied cottages it was not unknown for them to be evicted if their employer discovered they had voted against his political beliefs. My fellow author Bill Shepard's great grandfather was made homeless by farmer Fisk when two of his sons went into Newport from the Calbourne Farm where he worked, with a Liberal rosette on the horse's head.

Elections were sadly an excuse for outrageous hooligan behaviour to take place (much like that at Question Time in the House of Commons today) and depending on which newspaper you read, the blame was equally divided between the Tories and the Whigs. In June, 1841, in Newport, it was the Tories who got the blame locally in a report stating a brutal attack had taken place in Newport on unarmed men, women and children by a group of thugs wearing Conservative colours. A man named Bannister told how he was working at Cowes in White's Dock and had been told by his employer there was five shillings in it for him if he went to Newport. When he stated he was not of a mind to go he was told that if he did not, there was no more work for him. It was understood another man, named Ratsey, had also sent up from Cowes four hundred men, many who later noted that as four o'clock drew near, the time for polling to end, there was great excitement around the polling booth in the Market Place. Then the moment the poll closed a large body of powerful sailor-looking men with bludgeons in their hands, and wearing Tory colours on their chests, were let loose upon

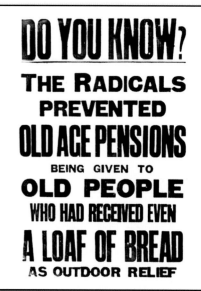

DO YOU KNOW?

THE RADICALS PREVENTED

OLD AGE PENSIONS

BEING GIVEN TO

OLD PEOPLE

WHO HAD RECEIVED EVEN

A LOAF OF BREAD

AS OUTDOOR RELIEF

the crowd. However, within minutes this group had been attacked themselves by the opposition's louts and soon some were unable to walk away. After thirty minutes there was no sign of any of them. It was said these Cowes invaders had been kept hidden in a pub owned by a Tory brewer in the town, who no doubt was a member of the Mew family, the pub being the Star Hotel in Lower St James Street.

In fairness, you could pick up another newspaper of a different political persuasion and a completely different account of the event would be reported. The result, if anybody is interested, was a win for the Whigs, Blake and Gisbourne, who obtained 277 and 279 votes each, while Martin and Hamilton got 268 and 267 for the Conservatives. As we can see by the numbers of votes cast, the right to vote, even nine years after the introduction of the Reform Act, was still restricted to a minority.

The voting for the General Election in 1847 to become the Island's MP was between John Simeon, of Swainston, standing for the Liberal Party, and Thomas Fleming of Binstead, representing the Conservatives. There were the usual claims of bribes, and threats being made, and one of the most respectable farmers on the Island was told that if he did not vote for Simeon he would lose his farm. The voting was at this time held over two days with

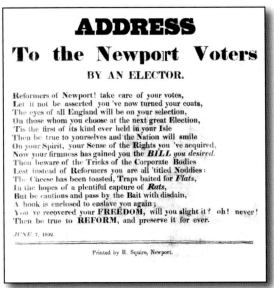

An election rhyme from 1832.

balloting taking place at Cowes, Ryde and Newport. Strangely, Mr. Fleming withdrew from the contest at the end of the first day, which was surprising as the final figures were only Simeon 476 and Fleming 373. During the day, two brass bands had paraded through Newport and when the result was declared the usual shenanigans commenced. A mob thundered at the gates of the Market House in Newport, intent on reaching the polling station and within seconds these gates were completely demolished. The mob then proceeded to head for the Tory haven, the Star Inn. Headed by two or three drunken old women, they soon smashed around twenty panes of glass with sticks and stones, by all accounts quite a normal activity.

Newport was not alone in being the venue for such disturbances and newspaper reports tell how both Cowes and Ryde engaged in similar riots at election times. Although not a general election rally there was another riot at Cowes on bonfire night 1869 when the locals carried a burning effigy of the unpopular landlord of the Fountain Hotel through the streets, one Tom Jones. When the police intervened the pontoon became like a slaughter house with hardly a square foot of ground not covered in blood. Later several local men were tried at Winchester and were each given four months in gaol. As stated, although not election related, it was certainly an anti-establishment demonstration.

Compare these scenes with today, and the widespread apathy that exists among the electorate is not that surprising when one considers how disgracefully Members of Parliament have behaved recently over what is commonly known as Brexit. However, we should never forget the sacrifices made by both men and women, like the Tolpuddle Martyrs and the Suffragettes in order to enable us to vote today, some sacrificing their lives for something that today many choose not to appreciate or, what is more likely, do not even know about. As Robert Lindsay would say in his role as Citizen Smith, "Power to the people!"

On, And Off The Rails

by Alan Stroud

A notice in the carriages of the Island's steam trains used to read, "Do Not Lean Out Of The Window" - a fairly sound piece of advice that was cunningly altered by boys of a literary bent to read, "Do Not Clean Soot Off The Window." The other helpful piece of advice offered was "Do Not Not Alight While The Train Is In Motion." Fair enough – who'd argue with that? Well as it happened, quite a few did....

It's hard to believe now, but long ago the Island had nearly 60 miles of railway lines - passing through every town and village that was worth visiting, and quite a few that weren't. It was a time when the train was the way to travel the Wight.

Most passengers were indeed happy to wait until the trains had reached the station before getting out. But not all of them. In 1906, Herbert Beard, a patient at Ventnor Hospital attacked another patient with a knife. The police arrested him but as the *County Press* explained, "A startling sequel occurred while the prisoner was being taken to Newport the next morning in charge of Police Sergeant Cass." The word 'startling' just about covers it.

At Ventnor West station the two men got into a compartment, sitting in window seats opposite each other. The train set off and after a brief stop at St Lawrence station it entered the tunnel that ran under the downs to

This is the St Lawrence end of the tunnel where Mr Beard did his disappearing trick. The tunnel mouth, now sealed up, can still be found in the undergrowth just off public footpath V81 in Seven Sisters Road.

Whitwell. There was no lighting in the carriages and the compartment was plunged into darkness. The train hurtled through the tunnel and emerged into the daylight, when Sergeant Cass was astonished to find he had the compartment all to himself - Mr Beard had vanished!

In the darkness, "inches from the sergeant's knee," he had managed to open the carriage door and jump from the train as it sped through the tunnel. Sergeant Cass heard the click of the door as it came to and puzzled, reached out for Beard but as the *County Press* poetically put it, "all he felt was empty space, for the bird had flown."

Once out of the tunnel Sergeant Cass pulled the communication cord and the train came to a halt at Dean Crossing on the Whitwell main road. With two passengers he made his way into the tunnel where he saw Beard sitting up, but by the time they reached him he was lying down, as if dead. He was carried on a stretcher to Whitwell station "seemingly unconcious" and put in the waiting room but the intrepid Sergeant Cass was suspicious. Everyone pretended to move away but the Sergeant crept back - to find Beard sitting up, none the worse for wear!

No chances were taken this time. When the next train came, Beard was locked in a carriage and taken to Newport police station. He appeared in court in April and was found guilty but "totally unfit to undergo prison discipline due to his state of health." Instead, he was sent to a workhouse infirmary in Lichfield. Not by train we hope, or he may well have never arrived there.

A few years later, two friends, Roy Taylor, 13, and Cecil Butt, aged 12, caught a train from Newport to Ryde one October afternoon in 1919. As the train raced through the Wootton countryside, the engine driver looked back to see a carriage door open, and then watched in amazement as Roy and Cecil got out onto the footboard and then, clinging to the handrails, made their way to another compartment, opened the door and got in. Flushed with success they went on to change compartments another three times before arriving at Ryde St Johns where they were apprehended. A few weeks later they appeared in court, the *County Press* reporting, "The fathers of the defendants said they were very good boys. They had thrashed them for their conduct. The Chairman said he was very glad to hear it. Taylor's father said the boys were out for a joy day. The Chairman: 'I suppose they get too much money.' Fined five shillings."

It's the early sixties and a train has just left Newport station on its way to Ryde and is about to enter the tunnel under Fairlee Road which is now today's pedestrian subway. Back in 1919, Roy and Cecil would be getting ready to take the air.

The next unscheduled departure from a carriage came the following year. On a freezing cold December night, a young man and woman, strangers to each other, were sharing the same compartment in a train from Freshwater to Newport. As it sped through the woods between Calbourne and Carisbrooke, the woman opened the door and hurled herself from the train into the darkness.

Calbourne Station in the 1890s

Under the headline 'The Girl Out of the Train,' the *County Press* reported, "Considerable alarm was caused on Tuesday evening when a gentleman passenger on the 5.30 p.m. train from Freshwater reported that a young lady travelling in the same compartment, had suddenly jumped from the train. Police and railway officials searched the line and found the young woman in a dazed state close to the platform at Watchingwell station. The lady from Newport, named Rayner, escaped with nothing worse than shock."

What went on in the carriage we shall never know. The *County Press* reported, "The incident gave rise to all sorts of rumours in Newport, but inquiries proved that her rash action was not due to any unpleasant incident. By her own admission the gentleman entered into quite ordinary conversation with her, but she became alarmed and felt impelled to get into another compartment. The gentleman said he was astounded to see her open the door and step out before he had a chance to stop her. The girl had a wonderful escape from serious injury if not death." Have a safe journey.

by Brian Greening

Newport of the 1860s would have been a dark, tough and grey place for the working classes, with long hours of work, if you could find it, bad housing, lack of sanitation and diseases such as typhoid and cholera. In a world of no cinemas, television or foreign holidays, an enjoyable day would be a street funeral parade before adjourning to one of the many public houses and seeing life through the bottom of a pint pot.

Funerals were often a grand spectacle.

Funerals in those days were dark, sombre occasions. It was only the wealthy that could afford a horse drawn hearse to convey the deceased to their final resting place. Mayors and councillors always had a good send off with shops closing their shutters, flags flying half mast and lines of men in long black overcoats and stovepipe hats following in procession to the cemetery. Being a barrack town, in Newport there were many spectacular military funerals that in addition to a horse-drawn hearse would be accompanied by a regimental band and hundreds of soldiers in full uniform. It was certainly worth coming out on to the streets to witness, to take one's mind off a cold, cheerless home in South Street.

Anything to do with the royal family, who lived just down the road at Osborne, also brought the inhabitants onto the streets, whether it was Queen Victoria passing through Newport on her way to Carisbrooke Castle or, in 1863, the marriage of her eldest son to a Danish princess. Her troublesome son, Bertie, later King Edward VII, who throughout his life maintained an appetite for food and the ladies, married that year. After a vetting procedure that took more than five years, and which began when she was just thirteen, it was Princess Alexandra of Denmark who was chosen. The

An arch at the junction of Castle Road and Carisbrooke Road, Newport, decorated for one of Queen Victoria's visits.

wedding took place in 1863 and towns and villages throughout the country set about making it a memorable day. Newport was no different, and on the wedding day the bells of St Thomas's started ringing at 7 am. At 10 am, the procession to divine service was led by the pupils of the girls' charitable Blue School in Crocker Street. They were followed by the National School's children with their flags and banners and wearing wedding

Celebrating Queen Victoria's silver Jubilee in 1887

Celebrations in 1902 at Snellgroves in Nodehill

rosettes. Then came the bands, led by a fife and drum, followed by the band of the IW Militia and the Volunteer Rifle Band. Behind was the mayor, Mr. Francis Pittis, the councillors in their robes and magistrates, police, members of the clergy and other dignitaries. After the service, around ninety of these dined at The Bugle Hotel before embarking on a decorated barge at the quay, lent by Messrs. Whites of the Cowes shipyard. Onboard was the band of the Isle of Wight Militia, heading for Cowes, where the mayor delivered an address to Cowes notaries.

What was interesting was how the town of Newport was decorated. It was the practice to erect decorated archways across the roads, on which would be a message of loyalty. There were several: one at the entrance to The Mall, another by The Bugle Hotel, one by the Guildhall, another at the lace factory at Staplers and a very good one apparently in Nodehill. A transparency presented to the town by Mr. Hobbs, of Coppin's Bridge, was fifteen feet high and eight feet wide. It depicted Britannia seated on a triumphal carriage surrounded by other figures holding the marriage contract, and sword of state. However, none could compare with that provided by local ironmonger Mr. Ellis, which showed a crown of brilliant diamonds in coloured stones, the Prince of Wales's plume, a star of brilliant stones bearing the garter motto, the royal arms encircled by a wreath of laurel and flowers, and all surrounded by flames of gas and coloured lamps. Along the parapet of his premises was a row of fir trees and silk flags of England and Denmark. Should a similar event happen today our Guildhall with be denuded of hanging decorations on account of 'health and safety.'

In the ensuing years, one man, Harry Guy, born at Cowes in 1862, came to know the royal couple well, after he became their boatman whenever they needed water transport. Harry wrote a book, detailing his relationship with the couple, mentioning the time he took the Princess by boat up the River Medina and then hired a carriage from Read's coaching

An arch at Hunnyhill, Newport.

establishment in Holyrood Street to take her and her friends to Carisbrooke Castle.

It was not unknown, however, for the media to criticize the royal family. A society magazine of the day was not impressed with the spectacle of the royal wedding of Princess Beatrice to Prince Henry of Battenberg at Whippingham Church on July 23rd, 1883, saying : "The royal procession from Osborne to the church was a truly contemptible affair. The carriages were simply ordinary vehicles such as people use for driving to the railway station and most of the horses were the sort of jaded steeds that would next week be dragging cabs up the hill at Goodwood." The reporter then went on to criticise the snobs who had paid half a guinea each to sit in a specially erected stand overlooking the road. They were grilled for two hours in the sun and finally saw nothing but a number of closed carriages that drove rapidly by. As they say, there is no pleasing some people.

by Alan Stroud

It only lasted two minutes eight seconds – but that was enough. In 1954, Bill Haley's 'Rock Around the Clock' let the rock and roll genie out of the bottle. Within a year, Elvis Presley had arrived and across the Island teenagers gathered in coffee bars to pay homage to that other arrival from America, the jukebox, while they drank their frothy coffee. Heady days indeed.

Local dance-hall owners saw the writing on the wall and the traditional dance bands were quickly elbowed out to be replaced by rock and roll or skiffle groups - and not just local ones. The list of well-known acts who appeared here from the mid-50s to the late 60s is a fairly impressive one. In the 50s it included Tommy Steele, Lonnie Donegan and Marty Wilde, not forgetting Newport's very own milkman-turned-pop star, Craig Douglas.

It was a slow start though. The *County Press* entertainments listings for March 3rd, 1956 reveals the dance hall favourites were The Music Makers, The Belvederes, Eric Galloway and his Band, and 'Kay Cavendish on the Keys'; catchphrase : "From Bach to Boogie."

That same week Mrs Rita Hobgen, a teenager of Ryde wrote a spirited letter to the *County Press*, "Sir, will some ballroom manager hold a dance where jive and bop is not objected to? If he did he would sell every ticket. Everywhere we go we are told 'No jiving.' Last week in Ryde we were told it is not respectable. If jive is not respectable some of the dancing that is all hugs and hot breath must be downright indecent, and no one ever bans that. As soon as jive is mentioned, our elders think of vice dens and opium. We aren't drug addicts, we're modern and we like to jive. Could someone give us 'kids' a break?"

And they did. The next year Lonnie Donegan came to the Commodore at Ryde, selling out two shows. He sang work songs straight from the Georgia cotton fields, ('shamelessly stolen', said some) including "Lordy, I shall not be moved" and "Alabamy Bound." On television Donegan, with no hint of irony, gave a surreal edge to

proceedings by performing these authentic slave songs while dressed in a Savile Row tuxedo and bow-tie.

One of the next attractions at the Commodore was Sabrina, a 21-year-old Stockport girl who enjoyed enormous fame and was, in the newspaper parlance of the day, a 'sex bomb' and 'sultry siren.' She was also described as a singer and actress, which were both fairly slender claims. The truth was, Sabrina was more widely known for her 42 inch bust than her vocal talents. In June 1957, at the height of her fame, she came to the Commodore and entertained the crowd with those perennial family favourites, 'I want a man, not a mouse,' 'It's better in the dark,' and 'Persuade me'. In a 1956 Goon Show, Harry Secombe, in the guise of a radio presenter, says, "Mrs Gladys Quimby would like to hear Sabrina sing ..... So would I."

In 1958, a singing milkman became the Island's first pop star when 17-year-old Terry Perkins from Newport won a local talent contest, changed his name to Craig Douglas and went on to have nine Top 40 hits. "Terry is an unassuming young man with a friendly smile," reported the *County Press*, "One of eight children, Terry, of 14 Prospect Road, Newport, is a milk roundsman." He wasn't for long. Rapidly leaving the crates behind him, Craig enjoyed a string of hits until in 1963 the Merseybeat revolution took place, sweeping away all that had gone before, and overnight, Craig and his contemporaries became yesterday's men. That year he appeared on the ITV show 'Thank Your Lucky Stars'. The Rolling Stones appeared on the same edition, and in his 1990 autobiography, 'A Stone Alone,' Bill Wyman recalled, "Craig Douglas had given our debut single a poor review and the Stones never forget anything. We knew he'd been a milkman so we went round the studios gathering up empty milk bottles and put them outside his dressing-room door with notes saying 'Two pints, please'. Furious, he reported us to the producers, who sternly reprimanded us." Craig, however, would have the last laugh. His pleasant singing voice stood him in good stead and he went on to enjoy a career spanning almost 50 years, and was still performing in 2011.

In 1964, Wyman himself trod the Island boards. The audience was keen. "About a dozen teenage girls, armed with blankets and hot drinks, waited all night outside the Esplanade Pavilion, Ryde, on Saturday to get tickets for The Rolling Stones concert on March 22. All the girls were in their early teens and produced written permission from their parents to the show organiser. They included Pat Searle, Brenda Hale, Linda Brown, Ann Michelle and Celia Lake."

In April 1965, the Beatles' single '*Ticket to Ride*' was released. Councillors at Ryde discussed whether there was any capital to be made out of what was thought at the time to be nothing more than a happy coincidence of wordplay. The *County Press* reported, "Mr. R. V. Bourn said there was a first-class opportunity for the publicity department to use a play on the title in their national advertising. One of his suggestions for an advertisement: "Why not take a ticket to Ryde this summer?" Well, had Mr Bourn known it, the title really was a direct reference to Ryde. McCartney and Lennon had visited Ryde several times in the early 1960s to stay with Paul's cousin, Bett. McCartney's 1998 book 'Many Years from Now' co-written with Barry Miles, relates, "Mike and Bett became the publicans of the Bow Bars in Union Street, Ryde, and Paul and John hitch-hiked down again to stay with them. It was a journey which would reappear, punningly, in the single 'Ticket to Ride.'"

Just as well they didn't go to Scunthorpe.

Accident at School Led To Man's Great Business Idea

by Brian Greening

A Kelly's Directory street directory is a fantastic window to a past local world. Here we can see names of businessmen who undertook skilled jobs that were appropriate to the time.

Around 1880 there would have been coopers, (barrel makers) saddlers, blacksmiths, boot and shoe makers and wagon and cart makers, all manual jobs that required learning a skill. For a few fortunate young boys an apprenticeship might occur, where the particular trade was learnt over a seven-year period. Let us move forward to around 1920 when we discover that in the Newport district there were no fewer than seven blacksmiths. I recall, too, the long established wagon and cart makers that were in Pyle Street, namely the Guy Bros, as well as Coombes, the saddlers in Nodehill.

The Witham family home in Pyle Street, Newport, with some of their products outside.

Frank Witham and his brother Ernest in 1915.

Recently, I was privileged to be given a few old postcards of another local firm dating back to around 1900, an enterprise that incorporated innovation with all the crafts. The family were the Withams, whose father came to the Island around 1880 from the London area and became the owner of nine river barges. However, his sons, led by James, the eldest, branched out into engineering, making invalid carriages and later moving on to sidecars for motor cycles. Their family home was at Pyle House, grand premises that in 2019 are the offices of chartered accountants, Harrison Black. The brothers had working premises at two venues in the High Street, plus a shop where later the Medina Café would reside, near to the Guildhall. Further repair premises would have been found on Coppins Bridge, so it can be seen they would not have been a business it was easy to ignore. The postcards I was given clearly show the range and also the quality of their products, that in the beginning were hand propelled invalid carriages. Many were testimonials sent by satisfied clients from all over England, as far afield as Nottingham and Bishop Auckland.

James Witham was the driving force behind this short-lived firm. Following an accident at school he was sadly confined to a wheelchair for the remainder of his life but he never let that hold him back. He was an intelligent youth and he developed a talent for writing articles for magazines before moving on to learn to type, a skill his sisters continued to teach for many

A satisfied customer with his crutches neatly stowed

years after his death. James put his disability to good use, as later he was instrumental in designing those self-propelled invalid carriages before moving on to motorcycles and sidecars. His disability made him aware of many of the details that might otherwise have been overlooked by an able-bodied person. He was well supported by his brothers, including Ernest, who, following being called into the army, served in India in the First World War. Sadly, James was to die in 1922 at the age of just forty five but in those few short years in business he had left an indelible legacy. Following James's death, Ernest was employed for over thirty years as a maintenance man for Southern Vectis. At its peak, the business employed around two dozen people. It was with a Mr Dingwall that Withams brought out the first Dingwall-Witham invalid carriage, which went on to gain not only a national but a world-wide reputation. Later James branched out into bicycle and motorcycle manufacture and maintenance. He became well-known throughout the Island, often to be seen sitting in his invalid chair to which he had fitted a Douglas motor cycle, operating the machine from the sidecar with special controls. He was a member of the IW Motor Cycle Club as well as being an enthusiastic photographer.

James Witham in his sidecar that was adapted to fit his Douglas motor.

The account of James's funeral tells us much about the man. He was buried in Fairlee Cemetery and those attending his funeral included many of the town's foremost businessmen, such as fellow engineer Bird Cheverton, who had premises in Lugley Street and whose firm had made carriages for Queen Victoria. Members of the Pittis, Black, Blake and Fred Trim families also attended, the latter becoming well known for his fruit and vegetable distribution business. Captain Brannon represented the Motor Cycle Club. Also attending were members of the Trojans Athletic Club, of which James had been a vice-president and, of course, his employees. Into his too short life this remarkable man crammed more than many who lived to be twice his age. However, the Witham name continued in Newport for a few more years. Although their cycle trade ended shortly after James's death, via his sister Queenie Witham, who taught typing at Pyle House for the next thirty years. One old Newport resident told how Queenie would cover her typewriter keyboard with an apron, thus ensuring she became able to type by touch. No easy lessons in those days.

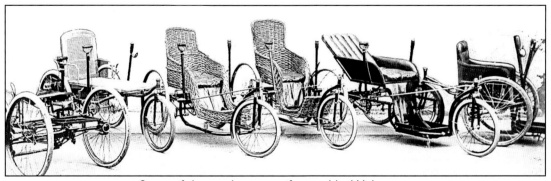

Some of the products manufactured by Withams.

THE BEMBRIDGE HARBOUR AFFAIR

by Alan Stroud

Many readers will remember Mark Woodnutt. He became MP for the Island in 1959 and for years was regularly returned with a large majority. In 1974 it all went spectacularly wrong when his 17,000 majority disappeared and he lost his seat by nearly 8000 votes. The cause of his sensational downfall was the 'Bembridge Harbour Affair.' Many will have heard of it but few know the exact details.

But surely the *County Press* reported the affair in great detail? Well, no. As a matter of fact they didn't. Like many newspapers, then and now, the *County Press* took a political stance and until 1973 it was an unashamed Conservative newspaper. Consequently, if Mr. Woodnutt, was ever to be criticised, it was not going to be within the pages of the *County Press*.

His downfall began with the closing of the Bembridge to Brading railway line in 1953. British Railways owned the harbour and 283 acres of surrounding land, and wanted to sell it. The Council set up two committees to find a buyer. Mr. Woodnutt chaired one and sat on the other. Their meetings, held in private and not minuted, recommended that a syndicate should be formed to purchase the site. Mr. Woodnutt then gathered some friends

Mark Woodnutt pictured in 1970.

and colleagues together to form just such a syndicate. His role was portrayed simply as that of a go-between, who would help the harbour pass to a group, who, Mr Woodnutt said at the time, "has no intention of acquiring the property for their personal benefit. It should not be allowed to pass into the hands of some speculator."

In 1968 the syndicate paid £24,000 for the harbour, a sum described by the *Sunday Times* in 1972 as "a bargain for them and an expensive deal for the taxpayer." Of that £24,000, only £14,000 was payable upfront, the rest standing on loan. Eyebrows were raised when just 18 months later, the syndicate recouped their entire outlay by selling just the station buildings for £16,500. Eyebrows went even higher when it was revealed that Mr. Woodnutt had quietly become a director of the company in 1966.

By 1970 the harbour was effectively run by Mr. Woodnutt and his friend, Major Selwyn, and in Company House documents they now valued their £24,000 investment at £150,000. A general unease began to grow about Mr. Woodnutt promoting the syndicate's case so keenly in 1962, only to quietly jump on board later as a director. The affair became a major talking point on the Island and eventually came to the attention of the BBC's *'Nationwide'*, a popular tea-time current affairs programme. Mr. Woodnutt agreed to an interview, to be filmed in his garden. He was asked a series of well-informed questions that he found 'impertinent' and he eventually brought the interview to a halt, angrily throwing his microphone to the ground and walking off-camera.

It was a fatal error - and from that moment on, Mr. Woodnutt's career began to unravel. Viewers who felt all along that something underhand had been going on had their suspicions confirmed, while many of those who had given him the benefit of the doubt so far, now withdrew it.

However, the *County Press* report of the interview mentioned nothing of the accusations levelled in it but concentrated instead, on what Mr. Woodnutt called the 'deplorable' behaviour of the BBC. Readers who had not seen the interview were left wondering just exactly what the deplorable behaviour was.

A Freedom Of Information request by the author to the BBC in 2011 revealed that the BBC still possessed a written transcript of the interview. A copy was obtained but for arcane copyright reasons the BBC will only allow a precis of the interview to appear, not the actual words spoken.

The report is introduced by Michael Barratt as a 'disturbing story.' The interviewer, Lynn Lewis, asks Mr Woodnutt why £10,000 of the £16,500 received for the station was diverted to syndicate members rather than being spent on dredging as promised. Locals claim no silt has been removed from the harbour, only shingle, which has been sold on. They are shocked to learn that the syndicate consists of not one but two companies, the site having been shared out between the Bembridge Harbour Improvement Company and Yarland Properties. Mr Woodnutt refuses to disclose the price paid for the harbour, commenting that some people are 'too damn lazy' to find it out themselves from company records. Lewis checks the company records - the figure is not there. Mr Woodnutt claims there were no other purchasers but Lewis reveals there were - including a higher bid of £35,000 which for some reason was not considered by British Rail. Mr Woodnutt angrily says he is 'not exactly a philanthropist.' The frustrated bidder of £35,000 is 'speechless' when told the harbour sold for £24,000. Mr Woodnutt says he is going to complain about Lewis, saying he has been bowled a 'bloody fast ball' and then throws his microphone to the ground. Walking away, he says he cannot carry on the interview tomorrow, or the next day, and then asks Lewis, 'Are you taking all this down?' There the item ends.

A year later, in a Council debate, Stephen Ross, the then Liberal candidate said, "To criticize Mr. Woodnutt and

Mr. Selwyn, supported, as they are, by a powerful weekly newspaper, is a task not undertaken lightly. Mr. Woodnutt took a very active part in Finance Committee. Was it intended all along that he would later join the syndicate? Is it in the best interests of this council that its two most influential members should be so deeply involved in planning matters." The *Sunday Times* revealed that the BHIC only owned everything below high water mark, almost exclusively mud and silt, while Yarland Properties owned everything above, that is, large amounts of land and buildings. The division was crucial. The terms of sale allowed the Council to compulsorily purchase the harbour if neglected, but the division of the property between two companies now meant that only the silted-up harbour would be available to them, the lucrative real estate having been stowed away beyond their reach in Yarland Properties. According to the *Sunday Times* of April 16, 1972, "The British taxpayer lost thousands, though precisely why is still not clear. British Rail declines to comment."

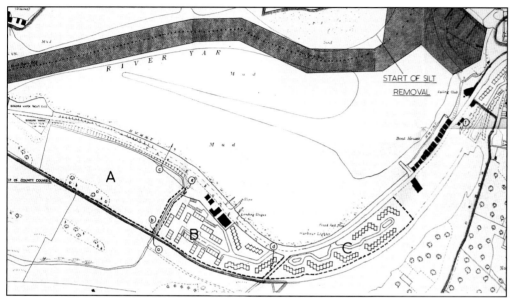

Shortly afterwards, Yarland applied for planning permission to build 120 houses on the land. The *Sunday Times* reported "Had they gained permission, the site would be worth almost £250,000." After a long public enquiry, planning permission was refused.

The affair continued to haunt Mr. Woodnutt. In July 1973, Willie Hamilton, MP, told the

The original planning application drawing showing 120 proposed houses on the two lagoons at the rear of Embankment Road. Today the lagoons form part of the RSPB nature reserve.

Commons, "He is deeply involved in the manner in which the land was sold to a syndicate of which he was a representative. It reeks of corruption and racketeering." The Island's voters agreed and delivered their verdict in the general election of 1974.

Sadly, just six months later, Mr. Woodnutt died, aged only 55, his *Times* obituary reporting, "His friends say he never recovered from his shattering defeat at the general election."

If the planning application had been successful, this lagoon and its partner, one on either side of the approach lane to Harbour Farm, would have been infilled to disappear under 120 houses.

WE HAVE LIVED THROUGH THE BEST YEARS

by Brian Greening

The title I chose for a book that I wrote a few years ago was "We Have Lived Through the Best Years," and it told a story of those, like me, born around 1940 and what life was like locally for them growing up in the next twenty years. In brief, my generation knew little of two world wars. On leaving school we had no difficulty obtaining a job that for many lasted a lifetime, we were able to purchase a house and on a lighter note we enjoyed an era of the best music ever written. Just think of all the pleasures our generation enjoyed.

Newport Grammar School group in 1929 with old Barton teacher David Martin, sitting front right.

How we sat and listened on the radio to a ventriloquist called Peter Brough with his dummy Archie Andrews. Not once did we see his lips move. We had Jack Warner on our black and white television playing Dixon of Dock Green and Bruce Seton starring as Inspector Fabian of Scotland Yard. We were in on the birth of rock and roll that saw the coming of Bill Haley, Gene Vincent, Fats Domino, Johnny Ray, Guy Mitchell and ladies such as Kay Starr, Doris Day and Teresa Brewer. Not forgetting of course the unforgettable Elvis Presley. We were around when food stopped being rationed and enjoyed Saturday morning cinemas when we would be entertained by the Bowery Boys, The Three Stooges and cowboys like Tex Ritter, Roy Rogers and Randolph Scott. We little boys fantasied too over Jean Simmonds, Susan Hayward and Rita Hayworth. Added to all this if you were born in my era you never saw once saw a doodle bug or had to take refuge in an air raid shelter. As I said, we lived through the best years.

Two things prompted this article. One was a visit with two of my friends to the local

Second World war soldiers coming back onto dry land.

ROLL OF HONOUR.

Sergt. **Deryck Abraham**, R.A.O.C., lost his life in France, September, 1944, after previous service in Norway and Iceland.

Flight-Lieut. **Lewis Bacon**, D.F.C., R.A.F., as the result of a flying accident in Scotland, February, 1945.

Flight-Sergt. **Alan Bunker**, R.A.F., in a raid on Bremen, June, 1941.

Engine Room Artificer **Herbert Burgess**, R.N., September, 1939.

Pilot Officer **Peter Burton**, R.A.F., reported missing on operations, December, 1942.

Engine Room Artificer **Richard Buxton**, R.N., when serving in the Mediterranean on H.M.S. Neptune, December, 1941.

Pilot Officer **Harold Chiverton**, R.A.F., in a raid on Dortmund, May, 1943.

Sergt. **Leslie Cox**, R.A.F., in an operational flight over Germany, September, 1941.

Kenneth Deacon, R.N., as the result of an accident in one of H.M. ships, June, 1942.

Sergt. Observer **William Elliott**, R.A.F., in October, 1940.

Pilot Officer **Richard Gerrett**, R.A.F., failed to return from an operational flight, Coastal Command, 1944.

Chief Engine Room Artificer **Leonard Gustar**, R.N., on H.M.S. Exmouth, January, 1940.

Sergt. Flight Engineer **David Hart**, R.A.F., missing after an operational flight with Bomber Command, March, 1943.

Sergt. Observer **John Harvey**, R.A.F., in attempting to bring back safely a badly damaged bomber after a raid on Northern France, August, 1941.

Sergt. **Albert Hawkins**, R.A.F., after air operations, April, 1943.

Flight-Sergt. Engineer **Patrick Hodgkinson**, R.A.F., after an operational flight over Germany, July, 1943.

Engine Room Artificer **Edgar Lavers**, R.N., missing from H.M. Submarine Triton, December, 1940.

Sergt. Observer **John Life**, R.A.F., in a raid over Germany, October, 1941. Is buried at Dornum, East Friesland.

Chief Engine Room Artificer **Heber McBride**, R.N., on H.M.S. Havant, 1940.

L.A.C. **Alfred Monk**, R.A.F., died in Java when a prisoner in Japanese hands, 1943.

L.A.C. **Cyril Morgan**, R.A.F., died while a prisoner in Japanese hands, August, 1942.

Sergt. Pilot **Hugh Nicholls**, R.A.F., failed to return from a reconnaissance of the Norwegian coast, June, 1940.

Police Sergt. **Denis Owens**, when on duty during a raid on Eastbourne, 1940.

Lance-Corpl. **Harry Parker**, R.A.P.C., reported missing when the s.s. Lancastria was sunk, June, 1940.

Warrant Engineer **Reginald Plumley**, R.N., on H.M.S. Hood, May, 1941.

Frederick Rae, when serving with the London Fire Brigade, October, 1940.

Sergt. Pilot **Bernard Riddett**, R.A.F., in 1942.

Petty Officer **Jack Russell**, R.N., on H.M.S. Hood, May, 1941.

Chief Petty Officer Steward **Cuthbert Sait**, R.N., on H.M.S. Galatea, December, 1941.

Sergt. **Alec Samuel**, R.A.F.V.R., on his 15th operational flight. Lost his life in France when returning from a raid on Milan, August, 1943, and is buried at Bernay in Normandy.

Gunner **Raymond Stark**, with the 2nd British Division, in Burma, 1945.

A.C. **Keith Stewart**, R.A.F., in October, 1941.

Sergt. **Alfred Taylor**, R.A.F.V.R., reported missing from an operational flight, December, 1941.

Sapper **Wilfrid Roy Twomey**, R.E., while being transported from Hong Kong to Japan as a prisoner of war

Warrant Officer Navigator **Robert Wendes**, R.A.F., killed in a crash near his home station in November, 1944, after having made 91 operational flights.

Engineer Room Artificer **Albert Westmore**, R.N., May, 1942.

Warrant Electrician **Vivian Wilks**, R.N., December, 1941.

Civilian Casualties.

Donald Abraham.
Dorothy Norris (née Wakely).
Douglas Sims.
Una Tuffley.
Marion Coster.

The roll of honour of old boys who had died in the Second World War, which appeared in the Newport Grammar School magazine after the war.

cinema to see the film 'Dunkirk,' which goes some way to telling the story of one of the greatest rescues of the century. What made it more personal was recalling the part played by ships based at our own Newport Town Quay and of their joining the flotilla of thousands to bring our soldiers home. Incidentally, this event is marked with a commemorative plaque on Newport town quay.

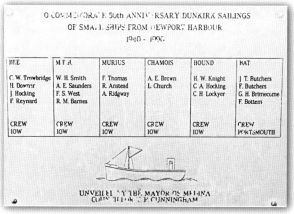

The plaque at Newport Quay showing the 'little boats' which took part in the Dunkirk evacuations

The second thing that brought closer the horror and despair many felt during the Second World War was reading a 1946 Newport Grammar School magazine that came into my possession. It happened to be the first produced by the Nodehill school following the end of that war. It listed the names and ranks of forty ex-pupils who gave of their lives in the service of their country.

It made me realise that had I and my two colleagues been born twenty years earlier our names, too, may have appeared on those pages. A brief analysis of these men tells us so much about the service they gave. The list gives us a list of the armed services they joined, of their ranks and the places where they lost their lives. Half of the forty joined the RAF, because being grammar school pupils they were considered brighter and were channelled there in line with national policy. They were lost on combat missions over France, Germany and Scandinavia. Two men were captured by the Japanese and died as prisoners of war. Eleven were serving in the Royal Navy and two were on board HMS Hood when she was sunk in May 1941 by the infamous German battleship, Bismarck. They were among the 1,400 that were lost. Another ex-pupil was on board the RMS Lancastria when she was controversially sunk by the Germans two weeks after the Dunkirk evacuation. We were still evacuating soldiers and civilians and severely overloaded the ship.

As a result, estimates of those who lost their lives ranged between 3,000 and double that figure, a vast number compared to the mere 1,500 who went down with the Titanic. Such was the extent of this loss of life the government withheld the story for several weeks, fearing the effect on morale the sinking would have back home. Poignantly, another ex-pupil was on board HMS Galatea when she was sunk in December 1941 by a torpedo from a German U-boat. My good friend Bill Shepard's brother, too, was serving on the Galatea and he sadly was among those drowned. Some may have gained consolation when it was learned that the U-boat was later rammed and sunk by an Italian torpedo boat.

Other ex-pupils were in the army and died in Burma or as prisoners of war or on the battlefields of France. Some were civilians, serving in the police and fire service during the London blitz. Those forty represented just a local snapshot of countless other stories replicated throughout the country. The fact that they were educated locally seemed, however, to bring their deaths that much closer. Eighty years later it can still bring a tear to the eye

"AN EXCUSE FOR DIRTY PEOPLE TO BEHAVE IN A DIRTY MANNER"

by Alan Stroud

On a Saturday night in September 1963, an open air jazz festival took place in the grounds of the Lakeside Inn at Wootton. A small affair, it attracted just 200 fans, but crucially, among them were teenage brothers Ray and Ronnie Foulk from Totland. Although the show itself was tiny, it inspired the two brothers to go on to produce the biggest music events that Britain has ever seen, the first Isle of Wight Festivals. They started with a small one-night event in a field in Godshill in 1968, where Jefferson Airplane and The Move entertained a crowd of nearly 10,000 and to their relief, made a modest profit. Encouraged by their success, the two brothers began to think about putting on a much larger festival the following year.

But who to get? With all the confidence that comes with youth, Ronnie and Ray thought big. In 1969 Bob Dylan was a counterculture icon with a mystique all of his own. He'd last been seen in Britain in 1966 when his electric performances shocked die-hard fans who labelled him 'Judas.' The furore, and a legendary motorcycle accident, drove him underground for the next three years and fans were now hungry for their hero to return. Ronnie and Ray decided he was just the act to headline their festival.

Dylan at his Seaview press conference

Getting Dylan to agree to perform wasn't easy but following dozens of transatlantic phone calls between his manager and a persistent Ray, a telegram finally arrived saying Dylan would appear. In a 2010 radio interview, Ray told Tom Stroud, "You could have knocked me down with a feather at that point. I had to sit down!"

Dylan's performance at Wootton would put the Island at the centre of a musical coup with massive, global appeal – except, that is, for the *County Press*, who, with just weeks to go, had yet to even mention it. On the Wednesday before the festival, Dylan gave a press conference at the Halland Hotel at Seaview. Reporters and TV crews from around the world descended on Seaview to get their first look at Dylan for three years but not the *County Press*. The editor, Mr Ash, the man with a world scoop on his doorstep decided the pop festival was of little interest to his readers. It soon would be.

150,000 hippies made their way to Wootton and the festival was a huge success. The following week's *County Press* referred to some festivalgoers as 'vagrant-looking individuals,' but conceded that there had been no trouble and that the police had praised the behaviour of the visitors. British Rail said, "We would be very happy to carry this crowd again. They were no trouble. We had less complaints about them than we receive about the usual Bank Holiday crowd."

The older generation on the Island were not happy with the disruption caused by what they saw as the 'sex and drugs and rock and roll' generation. They were determined that there would not be another festival. Mark Woodnutt, the Island's MP, was given space in the following week's *County Press* to pen an anonymous editorial. He wrote of "human beings who could leave such an indescribable scene of litter and filth behind them" and of "dangers to public health when 150,000 people crowd together for four days."

Over the next few weeks the Island's 'establishment' lobbied against festivals via the pages of the *County Press*, but ironically, they needn't have bothered, for the most outrageous, the most inaccurate, and the most unpleasant attacks on the festival and those who attended, came from *County Press* readers.

Will you be in the Isle of Wight on August 31st?

Bob Dylan will

These posters became a familiar sight across the Island.

The letters poured in for weeks. 'Disgusted' wrote : "The festival appears to be an excuse for dirty people to behave in a dirty manner to music. The resulting VD, illegitimate births and drug addiction will become obvious. The site is far less attractive than the most sleazy fairground and smells far worse. It is hoped the area will be sprayed with strong disinfectant to prevent the usual diseases that arise from insanitary, conditions."

Mrs Peggy M. Herbert-Gustar, of Wootton, wrote : "Now that the pop festival is over the truth can be told - the filth in our highways and lanes; shoplifting; partly built houses on this estate where rooms were filled with excrement and urine; drugs being sold; sex in public; and the noise so intense that we could not hear our television. To all this, the police turned a blind eye."

Mr B. Walter of Binstead took a different view : "Congratulations, young ones. You were well-mannered, courteous and pleasant to have around. You made us smile at your hippie gear, remembering when we also wore way out and crazy clothes. You brought a breath of life to an Island that seems to be peopled mainly by the old. I have every confidence in Britain's future. Come back again."

Some dirty people behaving in a dirty manner on the Saturday afternoon of the festival. Inset : A weekend ticket, which cost £3.25, the price of a double album, and a pack of lies from the Daily Sketch the morning after Dylan's appearance.

That wasn't a view shared by Councellor Alderman Minns. Rather unpleasantly he declared : "It was a pity that some of the younger Council members never saw Nazi concentration camps like Auschwitz. The smell at the festival site was similar, even though there might not have been the dead bodies." Ironically, the word Alderman means 'wise man'.

However, not every member of the older generation was that poisonous or jaded. The last word goes to a Mr J. Argles of East Cowes, who was indeed a wise man. He put things in perspective with this moving and thoughtful letter : "Many of the living dead of my generation are complaining about the invasion of the so-called Hippie people, who came in queer dress with packs and blankets on their backs, excreting in gardens and hedges, laying their women in the fields, stealing milk and eggs, and listening to a thunderous noise at night. I did the same when I was their age – the only difference being that I had a gun in my hand and with all the enthusiasm of youth we killed 3,500,000. The noise at night was somewhat different, but our elders told us that this was the right thing to do. Thank God this generation has rebelled and are only playing guitars. Youth will never be wasted on the very young this way."

The Greatest Pop Festival of the decade is now taking place here on the Isle of Wight
and coming to a climax with the ONLY MAJOR WORLD PERFORMANCE OF
BOB DYLAN IN FOUR YEARS.

IF YOU MISSED LAST NIGHT'S SHOW DON'T MISS TODAY AND TOMORROW AT THE ISLE OF WIGHT FESTIVAL OF MUSIC.

Come down to Woodside Bay immediately.

Today The WHO, MOODY BLUES, FAT MATTRESS, JOE COCKER, FAMILY, FREE, MARSHA HUNT & WHITE TRASH, PRETTY THINGS, GYPSY, BATTERED ORNAMENTS, BLODWYN PIG, BLONDE ON BLONDE, AYNSLEY DUNBAR RETALIATION, EDGAR BROUGHTON BAND, KING CRIMSON.

Tomorrow, Sunday BOB DYLAN AND THE BAND, RICHIE HAVENS, TOM PAXTON, PENTANGLE, JULIE FELIX, INDO-JAZZ FUSIONS, LIVERPOOL SCENE, GARY FARR, THIRD EAR BAND.

SATURDAY £1/5/-, SUNDAY £2

Tickets now available from Teagues, High Street, Newport; Teagues, Union Street, Ryde; Studio 4, Union Street, Ryde.

The only reference to the Festival in the *County Press* prior to the event was a series of large advertisements over the width of a whole page, placed by the festival promoters themselves, This one appeared on the Saturday of the festival.

THE CHANGING FACE OF NEWPORT

by Brian Greening

That Newport has changed in the past two hundred years is not disputed but it is difficult to conceive the time when beyond the boundaries of the town centre there were very few houses. In an article published in the *County Press* in 1885, an old resident recalled the Newport he knew in 1820. If we take the points of the compass as a guide he states that apart from Oyster Shell Cottages in what became Medina Avenue, there were scarcely half a dozen houses on the way to Shide. The two main premises were Mount Pleasant House, home to the Kirkpatrick banking family, and Shide farmhouse. Looking north from the bottom of Hunnyhill to the barracks at Parkhurst once again there were no more than half a dozen houses, and the situation was similar in Fairlee Road with Fairlee House being the largest property in the area.

We do have an excellent description of the scene looking from Carisbrooke Mall towards Carisbrooke village by John Albin in 1796. He described the journey he made from Carisbrooke Mall to Carisbrooke village and the Castle. It would have been a time before any houses were there and he tells of the uninterrupted views that were to be seen. In the beginning, Carisbrooke Mall was just two hundred yards long and, as Albin states, eight yards

Carisbrooke Mall and the raised promenade of which Albin spoke in 1796.

wide. It was a raised road where the ladies and gentlemen could promenade in their Sunday best, the ladies especially knowing they would not soil their long dresses in the mud and dust that existed throughout the town. Roads then were simply compressed gravel that became rivers of mud in wet weather and dust bowls in the summer months. This was Albin's description of the day: "The way to Carisbrooke Castle is through the High Street and Castlehold, taking the footpath called the Mall. On the left, it is partly shaded by lofty elms, under which some seats would be a desirable addition. On the right, it is open to meadows, which are backed by Parkhurst Forest. It possesses the further advantage of a good view of Mount Joy, Carisbrooke Castle, Carisbrooke village and Priory Farm. At the end of this walk is the horse road to the village of Carisbrooke and to the castle. Opposite is a narrow lane, which is the pass where it is said Sir Hugh Tyrrel, in 1377, defeated the French, who were on the march to Carisbrooke Castle. The lane is still called by the name it earned from that event, Deadman's Lane. Further on, the road divides, the left to the Castle and the right to the village, both of them carriage roads. At a short distance there is an agreeable path over the fields that continues by an easy ascent, till you arrive at the outer gate of the castle. This road is much improved and the waste ground, which is planted with various shrubs, will, in a few years, form an agreeable contrast with the surrounding fields and meadows."

An organ grinder and his monkey in Carisbrooke Mall in 1937

By 1850, the situation had changed dramatically and had you come to live in Newport at this time and were looking for a house, you would probably have sought the help of Mr Pittis, the estate agent, even then. Assuming you could not afford one of the imposing houses that were now being built on the Mall, he might have offered you a property in the grand sounding Paradise Row. Further investigation would have informed you this was the lane that joined the High Street with Pyle Street. Just how this thoroughfare obtained its name is unknown but in the years to come it would become home to 'ladies of easy virtue' and an area where police were called on a regular basis to resolve disputes. By 1846, those houses appeared to be attracting the wrong sort of resident. A young woman named Eliza Brading and her father, both described as 'notorious characters', were charged with being riotous and of assaulting a policeman. Their address was in Paradise Row, and while the father was fined 15 shillings (75p), the daughter, who was described as the 'dreadful Eliza', was given one month in the Bridewell gaol. Within living memory, there was a large property known as Castlehold House, complete with tennis courts, occupying the area to the right of the lane that later became Fowlers Garage and car showroom.

Deadman's Lane, that we know today as Trafalgar Road, formed a triangle with Carisbrooke Mall and West Street where there was at this time a cricket field. There were certainly a few beer shops there. In 1849, Charles Moon, who kept the Soldiers' Joy beer shop in the lane, was fined £1 for keeping a disorderly house. A year later, a soldier was charged with stealing an American clock, the property of the landlord of the Inkermann Arms beer shop in the same lane. It must have been a large clock as the soldier stated he had been given it by a man in the street and he thought it was a coffin. The Crab and Lobster was another beer shop in which a group of soldiers were attacked by two local men, one wielding a poker and the other a spade. In 1856, Theresa Austin, described as 'an old Irish Vixen and the terror of all her neighbours,' whose address was given as being 'in a poor district of Deadman's Lane,' was charged with brutally attacking a husband and wife for which she was remanded to Winchester Gaol for one month. Nearby was the unglamorous sounding Rag Row, which became Laundry Lane.

Scarrots Lane, too, would not have been an obvious choice; it was home to several slaughter houses. Cosham Street, later changed to South Street, was another area with more beer shops, plus the infamous Tontine public house where ladies of the night could always be found. Far better to consider a nice town house in an area such as Chapel Street, Union Street or West Street that were newly erected. If you wanted to be a little further out of town, this was a time when the houses in Elm Grove were being built. In Staplers Road, close to the then lace factory, houses were only erected in 1846. Mr Pittis described them thus, in typical estate agent language, "having commanding views of Carisbrooke Castle, in an elevated position with the advantage of being adjacent to the town without being liable to the peculiar burdens of the Island's capital."

Cosham House stood on the corner of South Street and Church Litten. In March 1777, an advertisement appeared in the *Hampshire Chronicle* offering it for let. It was described as being a large, newly built dwelling having a large entrance hall and staircase. It had two large parlours, a manservant's pantry, a very good kitchen, a washhouse and brewhouse plus cellar and wine vault. Upstairs, there was a drawing room and four good bedchambers. Outside, there was a large barn that could be used as a coach house, a stalled stable for six horses and a large back yard, all things that made it an ideal property for a genteel family.

Today, in Morrison's you will be walking on the site of Cosham House, which was demolished in the early 1850s. In more recent times such was the rough reputation of Gunville that a gentleman who moved there from Newcastle told his friends he lived in Carisbrooke Garden Village.

Newport High Street in 1897. On the right is the Antelope Inn, parts of which were incorporated into the elegant art deco Dabells shop which took its place in 1934. In an unforgivable act of corporate vandalism our council allowed BHS to demolish Dabells to replace it with a drab corporate building. BHS only lasted a few years but left the High Street with a permanent reminder of the damage they did in their brief time here, aided and abetted by a compliant and unimaginative council.

GIMME SHELTER

by Alan Stroud

Weren't the sixties good? We had pirate radio, the mini, colour tv.... And what was the other thing? Oh yes, we were all going to die in a nuclear war.

The problem was that Russia and America weren't getting on too well in the sixties and things got so bad that in 1963 the government issued a guide to surviving a nuclear attack. It was called 'Advising the Householder on Protection Against Nuclear Attack.' In it we were advised, and these are actual quotes, to "take a travelling rug if you have to flee your home," and "If you have to go outside, put on gumboots, a hat, and a coat done up to the neck." Well, who could argue with sound advice like that?

In 1965 the BBC made 'The War Game,' a drama filmed in documentary style, showing just what would happen to us in a nuclear war. Well, no sooner had they made it than they banned it, saying it was "too horrifying for broadcast." Apparently, we would have to put up with the real thing but we weren't allowed to see it on the telly first. In the event, it took them another twenty years to get round to showing it.

This is GPO engineer Bob Munsie, about to descend with the author into the Niton ROC Post in 1971. Located on footpath NT29 off Barrack Shute, the compound is totally overgrown today and the entrance to the bunker has been capped with cement.

In the mid-sixties, the government set up an early warning system to let us know when a nuclear bomb was on its way, the so-called 'four minute warning.' Bunkers were built across Britain and the Royal Observer Corps was set up, a volunteer civil defence force, who in times of trouble would man the bunkers, which were linked through the GPO telephone network.

An illicit photograph of the Niton ROC post looking skywards from the bottom of the ladder to the bunker.

On the Island, several ROC bunkers were built – at Freshwater on the golf course; at Newport in a field off Long Lane and at Niton in a field off Barrack Shute. They were kitted out with what were known as 'WB 400 receivers,' loudspeaker units connected to the national warning system. Receivers were also installed at police stations, hospitals, post offices and even a few rural pubs, all maintained on the quiet by the Island's telephone engineers. (Lest anyone should fear national secrets are being revealed here, the existence of the shelters and ROC posts on the Island is no longer classified; information about them is freely available on the internet).

In a past life as a telephone engineer I was occasionally involved in the maintenance of parts of the WB400 network.

Another furtive snap taken during our maintenance visit, this time of the 'Bomb Pressure Indicator'

Hidden in plain sight, this is one of the many nuclear air raid sirens dotted across the Island. This one was adjacent to Northwood Garage at Cowes.

There was a receiver in the White Horse Inn at Whitwell and in the early seventies I was sent there to service it. I discretely asked the elderly landlady where the receiver was and after gazing into the distance for a while she said, "Oh, you means that box thing over there!" and sure enough over there was the 'box thing' - on open display on a window sill in the main bar. Out of curiosity, when I finished the test I asked her if by any chance she knew what the 'box thing' was actually for. She gave me an old-fashioned look and said, "I haven't got a clue, my dear."

Message (a)	How Received (b)	Meaning (c)	Audible Warning to the Public			Notes (f)
			Equipment needed* (d)	Action to be taken (e)		
6 Attack warning **RED**	Warbling note followed by spoken message—"Attack warning **Red**" then steady tone interrupted at 4-second intervals for one minute (this is the remote control signal).	Imminent danger of attack.	Hand-operated siren. Power-driven siren.	**Hand-siren** sound the alert (wailing note) for one minute. **Power-siren.** If the siren does not operate by remote control, sound the alert for one minute.		**Hand-siren.** Act as soon as you recognise the warning—Do not wait for it to end. **Power-siren.** Wait for five seconds after the completion of the spoken message then if the siren is not sounding operate the local control.
7 Fallout warning **BLACK**	Calling signal (high-pitched pip tone) followed by spoken message such as "Fallout warning **Black, South Wales Twelve**".	Imminent danger of fallout.	Maroon.	If the warning message refers to your warning district, fire the maroon.		Ditto. If the meter at your warning point shows that radiation has reached 0·3 Roentgens per hour or more, fire the maroon whether or not the warning message has been received.
8 Attack message **WHITE**	Calling signal (high-pitched pip tone) followed by spoken message, "**Attack message White**", then steady tone for one minute. (This is the remote control signal.) (In this form the spoken message relates to all warning districts; if only some districts are affected their numbers will be given, for example "**South Wales Eleven and Twelve**".)	All clear, no further threat of attack or fallout.	Hand-operated siren. Power-driven siren.	If the message relates to **all warning districts or** to some including your **own:—** **Hand-siren**—Sound the all clear (steady tone) for one minute. **Power-siren**—If the siren does not operate by remote control, sound the all clear for one minute. If the message relates to some warning districts **excluding your own**—Take no action.		**BE SURE THE MESSAGE RELATES TO YOUR DISTRICT** **Hand-siren**—Act immediately the spoken message is received. **Power-siren**—Wait for five seconds after the completion of the spoken message then if the siren is not sounding operate the local control.

Supplied with every 'box thing' was an instruction card. This is an original one 'liberated' by the author. In chilling, official tones it details the warnings to be made to the public during a nuclear attack.

Things were in an equal state of precision readiness at the Niton ROC Post. The all-important circuit which would relay the life and death messages to the bunker was designated 'high-grade.' In reality, things were rather different, part of the circuit being carried on rickety old telegraph poles. The poles only just managed to stay upright in good weather; the chances of them surviving a nuclear holocaust were, frankly, nil. Added to which, the bunker was only twelve feet underground. Still, what did that matter as long as you had your travelling rug, gumboots and your coat buttoned up to the neck.

On a maintenance visit to the bunker in 1972, being young and reckless I took some forbidden photographs, including one showing the 'Bomb Power Indicator.' Ironically, if a nuclear bomb really had gone off nearby, by the time the needle of the indicator had moved into the danger zone the man in the bunker might just have had time to think, "Is it me, or is it getting hot in here?" before he was reduced to a handful of ash. Unless he had his gumboots on, of course.

Slightly more upmarket, underneath St Boniface Down there was a full scale nuclear shelter, complete with beds and food supplies. The complex occupied the large area underneath part of what was the Civil Air Authority's radar site. It was later refurbished as the IW Council's emergency command centre for use in time of nuclear attack.

At the time, the command centre's existence was a closely guarded secret known only to the workmen who built it, BT staff, most of County Hall and the entire population of Ventnor. Even a nuclear holocaust had its lighter side - in the 80s a member of staff put a hand-written notice up in one of the corridors. It read, "In the event of a nuclear attack, any member of staff unfortunate enough to witness the initial bomb blast should immediately bend over, place his head between his knees and kiss his ass goodbye."

Well, eventually Russia and the West kissed and made up, so in 1991 the centre was abandoned and sealed off with concrete slabs, leaving only the current air traffic control building. Apparently, there's no need for shelters and bunkers any more – the two most powerful nations in the world are now in much safer hands.

Hang on, that would be Putin and Trump wouldn't it? Right – where are those gumboots?

THE FIRE AT THE VINE BRANCH

by Brian Greening

It was in late September of 1881 that the picturesque village of Carisbrooke was awakened around midnight with the news that one of their public houses was on fire. This was the one known at the time as the Vine Branch that was situated close to the then Roman Villa and Vicarage situated on the left-hand side of Clatterford Road at its junction with Carisbrooke High Street. (Today upon this site is the popular Waverley public house.) At this time, there were, in addition to the public house that was owned by a Mr. Stephens, but tenanted by a Mr. Hewlett, also four thatched cottages on the site. The fire was discovered just after midnight and a messenger was immediately despatched to Newport to ring the fire bell. Within minutes the fire brigade were on their way to the scene with their horse-drawn vehicle but upon arrival found that due to there being no hydrant in the neighbourhood a supply of water was unavailable. A supply was, however, eventually found across the road and water was taken from a well in the yard of another pub, the Cutters Arms, but this was soon exhausted. Fortunately, there was little wind that might have spread the fire to other nearby thatched buildings.

Smoke was soon to be seen coming from a bedroom of one of the houses that adjoined the pub, one that was also used as a shop, and it was found that this room was used by the tenant to store bundles of faggots, (firewood) something that added fuel to the flames. The village policeman, Mr. Whitlock, was noted for his efforts to limit the damage and was later found in an exhausted state. During the fire, bottles of spirits were to be heard exploding. The occupants of the four cottages were rescued without any difficulty but for those sleeping in the pub it was a different story. The landlady and her daughters escaped via a ladder placed under their bedroom window, but her son was seen to make a perilous leap from a front bedroom down into the garden, a distance of some twenty feet, with a young child under each arm. A nearby stable escaped untouched from the flames. By morning all the buildings had been razed to the ground but thankfully there had been no loss of life. Both the contents and the pub buildings were covered by insurance, but sadly not the cottages. Within two years a new pub was built on the site and became known as the Waverley, the self-same one that stands there today. Its name owes more to the man who had it rebuilt, Mr. Wavell, than any connection to a ship of that name.

It was in 1914 that the Waverley had some distinguished guests in the form of a group of suffragettes who stayed there, after they had had to leave the Bugle Hotel in Newport High Street where they were jeered and abused by a rowdy mob.

The Castle Hotel that opened around 1880.

Red Lion Hotel staff possibly waiting for a horse drawn carriage to arrive with guests.

For many years very close to the Vine Branch, just a few yards up the hill, was the Old George, another local beer shop. No doubt its business suffered from the proximity of the Vine Branch but it was there in 1847 that the landlord Mr. Dennis had his license renewal refused because of disorderly conduct on the premises.

Carisbrooke has had several public houses that bordered the main street. Some it appears attracted noisy clients and the Cutters Arms was frequently in the news for selling beer and allowing singing on the premises after hours. Such was the case in 1845 and a year later the then landlord, William Guy, was fined 25 shillings for using inaccurate measures. The Red Lion and the Castle Hotel were virtually next door to one another in the High Street. The Red Lion pre-dated the Castle Hotel and it was used as early as 1852 by the bell ringers from the nearby church for their annual get together. As Carisbrooke grew in popularity as a tourist attraction, the Castle Hotel was opened in 1878 and was only finally closed in 1969. Across the road on the corner of Castle Street there was the Bugle Inn that at one time had steps up to the front door. There was a fire there in 1899 but little damage was recorded.

No mention of Carisbrooke pubs could be made without naming the still trading Eight Bells that had to its rear a large pond that enabled boating and fishing to take place. It also boasted a bowling green and regular matches were contested there often against mainland opposition as in 1885 when the visitors were from Fratton in Portsmouth. The touring Australian cricket team are known to have dined there too. Newport Choral Society held their dinners there as early as 1829 and it was annually used for flower shows that specialised in dahlias and ranunculus, the latter being related to the buttercup family.

There was sadness too in the village in 1844 with the demise of a Mrs. Pragnell, a lady who had for many years sold fruit at the gates of Carisbrooke Castle. A young relative returned from the wars with a pocketful of back pay and went into the Eight Bells and treated the villagers to a drink. This included his elderly aunt who apparently imbibed too much. Her husband, who was similarly intoxicated when he went to bed, woke up the next morning to find her quite dead, lying on the floor beside their bed. The village, it seems, could never be described as dry.

The old Bugle pub that was on the corner of Castle Street, with steps that could prove dangerous after an evening spent supping ale.

THE SINGLE TICKET THAT MADE A RETURN JOURNEY

by Alan Stroud

On a quiet afternoon in April 1889, a Cowes-bound passenger approached the ticket office at Newport railway station. He was served by 21 year-old Christopher Mursell who sold him a single ticket, number 2658, for the 6.24pm train to Mill Hill station at Cowes. On arrival there he handed the ticket to the young porter waiting on the platform. Two hours later, the same man, a Mr Lawler, returned to the Newport booking office to make another journey. He was again served by Mursell and bought a ticket for the 8.47 to Mill Hill. Remarkably, it was also numbered 2658. Somehow this ticket, collected at Cowes a couple of hours before, had found its way back to Newport booking office, to be sold to him a second time.

Mill Hill station, Cowes, and stationmaster in the early 1900s, complete with (re-created) ticket.

Mr Lawler was quite sure of that for two reasons – Firstly, because he had taken a note of his ticket number, 2658, and secondly, he had noted it because he was a private detective hired by the Isle of Wight Central Railway "to detect a fraud which they thought was being perpetrated upon them." Mr. Lawler had also noted that the curious coincidence that the young man who had collected his ticket at Mill Hill station was none other than Christopher Mursell's brother, Robert.

And so it was that a few weeks later Christopher appeared in court at Newport Guildhall charged with 'embezzling monies' where tellingly, he was described as "lately employed as a booking clerk." In the words of the *County Press*, "The case excited great interest and there was a large attendance of the public."

Mr. Fardell, prosecuting, said the case was simple – "It was the duty of the booking clerk to enter in the train book, every ticket issued and to enter the monies. On the 12th April, prisoner stated by his train book that ticket 2658, for Cowes, was issued at 4.15. The next train was at 6.24, and prisoner stated that for that train he issued no ticket. For the 8.47 train he said that he issued a ticket numbered 2659 - but what the prisoner stated was not what had happened," insisted Mr Fardell.

Mr Lawler then gave evidence that despite Mursell's claims, he was sold 2658 for the 6.24 train. "I proceeded to Cowes and gave the ticket to the young man there and returned to Newport by the next train. On arriving I saw that man, prisoner's brother, on the platform.

Mr Fardell cut to the chase : "The prisoner's brother was stationed at Mill Hill and it was part of his duty to collect tickets there. It was a curious fact that that brother came back to Newport by the same train as Mr. Lawler did, and on arriving at Newport Mr. Lawler saw him walking in the direction of the booking office. Mr. Lawler returned at 8.47 and asked for a ticket to Cowes. The ticket issued to him was 2658 - one of the tickets which, according to prisoner's own entry in his train book, he had already issued for the 4.15 train."

Mr Fardell went for the kill : "If Christopher Mursell was in a position to issue it again at 8.47, that ticket must have been collected at Mill Hill and brought back to Newport. How? I say they were collected at Mill Hill by prisoner's brother and brought back by him to Newport and reissued by the prisoner."

Christopher's brother, Robert, then took the stand. He needn't have bothered really; an attack of amnesia saw

Newport station in the late 1890s, looking much as the Mursell brothers would have seen it.

to that. "I don't remember if the tickets by the 4.15 train were collected at Mill Hill.... I don't remember if I travelled to Newport by the 7.20 train on the day in question.... I don't remember if I was in Newport that evening."

Mr. Fardell tried to jog Robert's memory: "Did you bring anything up from Cowes on the evening referred to? Witness : I decline to answer. The Chairman : Is it on the grounds that it may incriminate yourself that you decline to answer? Witness : It is."

Herbert Simmons, traffic manager, told the court, "I summoned prisoner into my presence. I said 'Did your brother bring you back any tickets from Mill Hill?' Prisoner said 'No.' I then said 'Did you issue 2658 over again?' Prisoner said 'I have no knowledge of it.' I said 'You issued 2658 by the 4.15 train. This gentleman (pointing to Mr. Lawler) purchased it from you at 8.47.' Prisoner said 'I cannot account for it.' I said he must consider himself suspended." Mr. Lamport, defending, said, "There was an entire absence of anything that could suggest crime. It was said that the prisoner misappropriated the sum of 9d. Had they proved it? No. In spite of the efforts of this company to prove his client's guilt, he was no more criminal than any other person standing in the Court that day (applause)."

So there was the evidence - Two brothers perfectly placed to commit the crime, a convenient loss of memory by one of them, coupled with the damaging admission that answering the prosecution's questions might incriminate him.

The magistrates took just twenty minutes to consider their verdict. The Chairman then delivered it to a hushed courtroom. "Christopher Mursell, the Bench are of the opinion that there is not sufficient evidence to convict you of this charge, and you are therefore acquitted." At that, "the courtroom erupted with cheers and loud applause from friends and relatives of the two boys."

Christopher, probably as surprised by the verdict as anyone, left the court to return home as an innocent man. If he went home by train, let's hope it wasn't on a second-hand ticket.

Newport in 1972. The station is just about to be demolished to make way for Medina Way which opened in May, 1975.

by Brian Greening

When I was growing up in the fifties, boot scrapers were legacies of the days when unsurfaced roads were seas of mud. A look around the town even today will discover many fine examples that still exist. One good example can be seen in the wall of a house between what until recently was Beavis and today's Farm Fayre shop in Nodehill. There are several in Trafalgar Road and certainly two more in the wall near County Hall. There are

The Cyclists' Touring Club emblem on the wall of The Wheatsheaf in Newport.

The sign for Self's Pie Shop in Newport High Street above today's 'Wheelers Solicitors.'

many other 'signs of the past' and in a short tour of the town many can be highlighted. Opposite the Guildhall, outside of Legends, glance up and across the road, and you will be rewarded with a painted advertisement for Mr. Self, the original maker of those hot, peppery pies. Mr Self advertised himself as the 'Pastry Cook', and this was the original home of his 'Noted pie shop'. Entering Watchbell Lane between Calvert's Hotel and Holyrood Street there is a metal sign asking that persons refrain from riding bicycles and tricycles through it. It is signed by Mr. Ross Pratt, Newport's town clerk, in 1937. A short walk to Lower St James's Street, and in the gable of what is Newport Social Club is the smiling face thought to depict Bacchus, the God of wine. Around 150 years ago this building was a porter and wine store. Pedestrians in Post Office Lane, near its junction with the High Street, will see a handrail above head height and immediately below it, carved into the brick wall, a 'toe hole' to accept a man's boot cap. It was either for a policeman to pull himself up and look in through the window at a time when

Newport Reform Wharf, founded in 1832, is marked today by this section of wall on Coppins Bridge

it was the Post Office sorting room, or a means for the postmen to alert their colleagues to open the door after completing their rounds. Up the High Street, as far as the Castle Inn and just down Mill Street on the left-hand side, in the brickwork can be seen the remains of the words, 'Commit No Nuisance'. The story goes there was once a side entrance to the Inn and many men used it to gain access to the pub's toilets. The fed-up landlord took to locking the gate and desperate individuals then simply used an alcove across the road to relieve themselves, hence the message in the wall. Years ago there were two public urinals that had little more than a cast iron screen to satisfy public decency, one at the bottom of Hunnyhill and another against the wall of the old malt house opposite the Medina Railway public

Bacchus, the Roman god of wine, above Newport Social Club.

house. What did they have in common? Both discharged straight into Lukely stream. The toilet block on Coppin's Bridge, on the other hand, drained straight into the River Medina. With an increasing population and St James Square becoming the arrival point for bus passengers there was a scheme proposed for an underground toilet between the Victoria monument and the County Club, whose well connected members soon made sure that this proposal was knocked on the head.

Exit New Street into Pyle Street and directly across the road there is a rough wall behind which was once the Town Pound, where stray animals were kept. According to Bill Shepard, this dated back to the 16th century. Up the road, the first part of Carisbrooke Mall, built around 1810, went for a distance of 200 yards and was said to resemble a pier extending out to sea. It was raised above the level of the often muddy road to enable ladies to parade and 'promenade' in their voluminous dresses. On the wall of the Wheatsheaf Hotel, there is a sign that

This 'Commit No Nuisance' sign is still visible on the wall in Mill Street at its junction with Newport High Street

told cyclists that the landlord would offer reduced terms for members of the national Cyclists' Touring Club.

Angled stones embedded at the base of the walls of narrow passages stopped cart wheels damaging them. Examples can be seen in old photos of Town Lane and Carisbrooke High Street and today in both Trafalgar and Chain lanes. A barely noticed metal ring in the kerb stone outside

what was once the Lamb Tavern in St James Square was used to thread a rope through so barrels could be lowered into the pub's cellar. Few seeing that today would know its raison d'etre. Another reminder of Newport's past is the portion of wall that still remains on Coppins Bridge that commemorates the granting in 1832 by Newport's Corporation to the Churchwardens and Overseers of a thirty year lease on nearby land to create a wharf where the poor could collect coal brought up to this point by barges that could be delivered without incurring wharfage dues. 1832 was indeed the year of the first Reform Act that extended voting rights to a greater number of townsfolk. The wall and stones are visible at the High Street end of the pedestrian crossing that leads to Barton Raod.

At the top of West Street, as it joins Trafalgar Road, into the wall of what was once H.W. Morey's offices, is a stone tablet recalling that on that site was once a school known as Portland House Academy. It originated in Portland Street in 1865 but later moved to this site, finally closing its doors in 1928. It was a school at which many eminent Newport citizens started their schooldays.

The 'toe hole' and hand rails in the wall along Post Office Lane.

Mr Ross Pratt's 1937 sign in Watchbell Lane.

Snakes Alive! - Or Dead, As The Case May Be

by Alan Stroud

To mix metaphors, snakes are not everyone's cup of tea - our slithery friends are most definitely an acquired taste; however, County Press editors over the years have always been quite fond of them. Space could always be found for a snake story – if it involved adders, even better.

In April, 1887, the normally level-headed *County Press* seemed to believe in an urban myth when they wrote, "A boy named Wheeler was on Rew Down on Tuesday, when he was badly bitten by an adder with alarming consequences. The downs were searched to find an adder to procure the fat to apply to the bite. One was found and the fat put on, but it is feared the remedy has come too late."

In July 1900, it was a grass snake that caught the Editor's eye : "A very fine specimen of the common harmless ringed snake (*Tropidonotus natrix*) was killed in the riverside grass on Tuesday by several boys, and its exhibition at premises in the High Street aroused considerable interest. Its length was 3ft. 6in. and it was found to contain the abnormally large number of 40 eggs, which, about as big as chestnuts, are strung together sausage-like. The reptile has been secured by Mr. Percy Wadham, the taxidermist, who possesses an even larger specimen of the species, which was caught at Dodnor several years ago and is 3ft. 9in. long."

Percy became very well-known over the years, not only for his stuffing skills, but also as an expert naturalist and angler and made countless appearances in the *County Press* , including this one in 1922 : "A fine specimen of an adder, 2 ft. long, that was killed at Cranmore has been exhibited in our window this week. Mr. Ridett, who caught it, says "It is often said that they never exceed 1ft. 9in. in length," but Mr. Percy Wadham, of Newport, says: "The average length of Isle of Wight vipers is about 1ft. 9 in., but I have seen specimens over 2ft. 3in."

Percy Wadham, taxidermist extraordinaire, greeting one of his clients.

Percy with another piscatorial conquest

This startling photo appeared in the *County Press* in March 1939. The original caption read, "Adders caught as a hobby by Mr. C. Cassell and Mr. Banting of Shanklin. It is estimated that if these had been allowed to breed they would have produced 330 offspring."

To go off at a slight tangent, an article from July, 1900 provides a poignant footnote to Percy's activities and tells a tale of something that hasn't happened for many a year : "An enormous trout, scaling 3lb. 9 oz., one of the largest ever caught locally, was recently landed by Mr. Percy Wadham from the pond at Town Gate. This fine fish, which had for some years eluded capture by local Waltonians, at last yielded to the temptation of an early morning bait, and it will be duly preserved, as it deserves to be, as a fitting object for the admiration of those interested in matters piscatorial." In the next ten years many gravelled Island roads were tar sprayed with the arrival of the motor car. Cedars Hill was sprayed and the run off from the next rains killed every fish in the Lukely. Percy was outraged and achieved moderate national fame by becoming active in a national campaign, via the *Fishing Gazette,* for the regulation of chemicals released in rivers.

Back to snakes, and in March 1935 under the headline "Bitten By An Adder," the *County Press* reported : "Raymond Ryall, the 5-year-old son of Mr. and Mrs. F. Ryall, of Mottistone Farm-cottages, is now recovering in the County Hospital after being critically ill during the week-end as a result of an adder bite. The boy was playing in the backyard and he apparently trod on the adder, which bit him in the calf of the left leg. By the evening the poison had so seriously affected him that he was taken to hospital by Mr. Jackman of Mottistone Farm." Happily, Raymond recovered; not so the adder, apparently, the *County Press* going on to report : "Mr. Jackman and his sons kept watch at the spot where the boy was bitten and on Monday they shot a pair of fully grown adders."

It wasn't a good time for grass snakes either. In July 1949, the *County Press* reported, "Mr. Fred Short of Alderbury Road, Newport, killed a 4 foot long grass snake in his garden on Sunday. It was not recognised as a

A black adder sunbathing near Afton Down golf course in the summer of 2017. Photo : A nervous Alan Stroud.

harmless snake and because there were children nearby, it was killed with a blow from a spade."

The next adder to go was killed by a blow from a shoe, in summer, 1950 : "Mrs. E. Dark was bitten by an adder on Tuesday. With her friend, she went for a walk across Headon Warren, where they sat down for a rest. The adder, about a foot in length, bit Mrs. Dark in the left forearm. Showing commendable presence of mind, she crushed the reptile to death with her shoe, applied a tourniquet above the wound and walked to Totland in search of a doctor, who treated her with anti-viper serum. When the tourniquet was removed Mrs. Dark suffered rather badly, and became delirious. On Wednesday morning, however, she was making a good recovery, although still in great pain."

In the summer of 1953, an adder was run over by a motorist on the Bleakdown Road. According to him it was three foot long. The *County Press* was sceptical, noting : "Mr. Fred Cole, of Blackgang, who has caught over 200 adders, and in pre-war days sent them alive to Germany where their venom was extracted for medicinal purposes, informs us that he has never caught one larger than 29 inches." The motorist was stung to the core and insisted in a follow-up letter that the adder was definitely three foot long – He had photographed it and would send a copy as proof. The photograph never arrived.

But a letter from Mr Ralph of Cowes did – and talk about whoppers! "Sir, my opinion is that there are some reptiles of abnormal size here. On one occasion, about 50 years ago, I came upon a nest of 165 grass snakes about nine inches long, and when working at Haslett Farm one day, I heard a loud hissing and saw a huge snake lying over a hedge, about 6 to 7 feet long. J. H. Ralph. 4, Egypt Cottages, Cowes." And no doubt Mr Ralph spotted all those dragons and unicorns as well.

Finally, in March 1966, under the headline "Thirsty Adder Meets Its Doom," came this beautifully written story: "Patrons are always assured of a friendly welcome at the Sportsman's Rest at Porchfield but the exception proves the rule. On Monday, Mrs. Jill Tilbury, wife of the licensee, Mr. John Tilbury, had a shock when she saw the first customer of the morning - an adder. By way of introduction the visitor flung back its head and hissed. Mrs Tilbury called for her

A common adder. Taken from Oliver Frazer's *'The Natural History of The Isle of Wight'* by kind permission of Colin Pope.

husband, who, armed with a mallet, called a hasty "Time, gentlemen, please" for the adder. With the introductions complete, Mr. Tilbury transferred the adder to a large jar - tangible evidence for any friends who might otherwise have doubted the story."

After all that, it's worth bearing in mind that since 1950 only one person has died from an adder bite in the UK. In the same period 61 people have died from bee stings!

by Brian Greening

My grumpiness is well known locally and goes back to the days of my friendship with the much-missed Keith Newbery, that scourge of Southern Vectis, the County Council and any local Freemasons. The reason for his dislike of the latter has been given that as a baby he was bitten by one while still in his pram but this is untrue, the real reason going much deeper. Personally I hate change. For example, I dislike going into a supermarket to find the counter where I always purchased my slices of brawn is now selling cat and dog food, or where I normally found the toilet rolls is now inappropriately selling white spirit, paint scrapers and sandpaper.

God's Providence House, circa 1910, with the Green Dragon in the background.

This got me around to thinking just what any returning Newport-born resident, who had left the Island in their teens, would make of the town today. It is doubtful they would be naive enough to believe nothing would have changed in the intervening years but just how much would they miss of their childhood days? Certainly, they would miss the trains and the disappearance of the railway station and that great metal bridge at the bottom of our High Street. Gone too, they would discover, is the cattle market that was in South Street where I and many other children would make for every Tuesday to see

and touch the sheep, pigs, chickens and calves and even occasionally see a dog tethered up to be sold. Gone too would be the hot dog stall where that new delicacy of the time would have been on sale. The cattle market was opened on September 11th, 1928, by the mayor, Cllr W. Blake, after being in St James's Square from around 1532. Sir John Oglander recorded that around that time the Corn market was held in St Thomas's Square while the beast market was in St James's Square. He claimed neither was paved until 1654 when, with the proceeds of the sale of goods of a suicide victim, the former was paved, using the sum of £24 3s 2d raised. The new South Street cattle market was at the time a splendid construction, the frontage of it being built by using the bricks and tiles saved from the Green Dragon public house, that had stood opposite God's Providence House for more than two hundred years and commenced its demolition in 1924. It seems inconceivable to imagine that Church Litten and Town Lane were once no wider than the width of a single horse and cart. By 1924, Church Litten had already been

Mayor John Curtis Millgate and his daughter, Christabella.

widened and Town Lane was planned to be next, increasing its width from less than twelve feet to thirty-seven feet. However, in early 1900 there had begun the introduction on to our roads of motor cars and very soon, as now, they began to dictate any changes that were to take place within the town. With Church Litten and Town Lane widened, the next target for demolition would be God's Providence House. In 1924, God's Providence House was tenanted by a Mr Wells, selling all forms of crockery. Then, in 1927, there was a letter printed in the *County Press* from a member of the Hobart family, who, at the time, lived at Standen House. In his capacity as a senior member of the Chamber of Commerce, he described the house as being dilapidated, of having no historic interest to recommend it and said it stood in the way of a much needed improvement scheme. (No doubt he had a car)

A year earlier, the Council had talked of purchasing the property to use as a museum or possibly a mayor's house. Indeed, when the new market in South Street was opened in 1928, the Mayor even then commented that the recent change the new cattle market had made to the town was progress, and went on to say antiquity was all very well but it must give way to modern demands and he wished that God's Providence House had been removed. Then, riding to the rescue came two local eminent architects in the form of Percy Stone and John Curtis Millgate. The latter was Newport's mayor on three occasions and when, in 1911, he was so honoured, he took as his mayoress his twelve year old daughter, Christabella, as sadly his wife had died in childbirth in 1903. Indeed, Christabella took the same position on the two following occasions her father was mayor. These two "knights in shining armour" secretly purchased the property for £850 and then had it scheduled by the Ministry of Works as an ancient monument that stopped any destruction or alteration of the building. Indeed, Mr Millgate did a similar

The Mission Hall in South Street, adjacent to the Market site.

deed when the Roman Villa at Cypress Road was beginning to be vandalized, so he purchased this too, covered it over and preserved it for future generations to enjoy. Personally, I applaud our two architects for their preservation efforts. I do not often go along with wasteful demolition of our ancient buildings and wish those that followed them had put the same sort of effort into preserving Hazards House, once said to be the oldest house in Newport, when in the early 1960s it was demolished to eventually make way for the County Hall extension, a building that today I would welcome seeing the end of.

Another thing that has also disappeared is the many milestones that were once all around the Island. Hilda Corbett, an old Gatcome resident told how there were once four marking the distance from Newport to Chillerton. The first was near the cemetery gates in Whitcombe road, the second in what is now a layby just past Whitcombe Manor, a third on the slight rise just past the entrance to Gatcombe and the fourth outside Chillerton club. Road widening, with no thought given to the past, has accounted for most disappearances.

The outside of the cattle market that was once in South Street.

by Alan Stroud

It was early 1938 and things were not looking too good. There was ominous talk of massed hordes of invaders from across the sea who would be soon landing on our coasts. Yes - Holiday camps were coming to the Island.

The letters to the *County Press* began almost immediately. "Dear Sir, holidays in holiday camps with little clothing, plenty of noise, and few restrictions seems to satisfy a popular demand and bring considerable profit to the promoters. The camps will undoubtedly be supplied with provisions from the mainland; clothes are unlikely to be purchased locally and any demand for souvenirs and cheap cosmetics will probably be met at the camp canteen. Whitecliff Bay is threatened with invasion by strange hordes and at Wootton, an equally undesirable camp leads past a number of good class private residences. In the West Wight we already have several of these camps, the inmates of which march about quiet country lanes making night and day hideous with their community songs, some of very doubtful taste. I am, Sir, 'Island Resident.'

The next week brought more of the same. "These camps are a menace in every way to all the decent residents of the Island. The best part of the year is ruined by this hostile invasion of campers who infest every bathing beach with their undesirable presence and pervade our quiet streets and lanes with their raucous shouts and so-called 'singing.' Their manners are negligible, and they have no consideration whatever for others. It is high time the authorities took measures to suppress any further depredations. Yours faithfully, Fellow Island Resident."

This cartoon appeared in the County Press in early 1938, subtly fanning the flames of the holiday camp debate.

Frank Boyce, of London S.W.13, perhaps a 'camper' himself, stuck up for the infesting hordes : "Sir, — Your correspondents are greatly biased. The camps are large employers of labour and their clients, about 20,000 last year, spend a lot of money locally. The visitors are not 'strange hordes,' but mostly teachers, civil servants, office workers, etc. I can assure him that he will not be attacked with battleaxes — they may be armed with nothing more than 'cheap' cosmetics."

Clara Ross, of Green Gables, Freshwater Bay, was concerned about "decent-minded people" and the local youth being subject to "corruption from outside" : "The Island is so small that undesirable visitors make themselves heard, seen and felt in a way which might not be the case in a larger area, where they could disport themselves without annoying decent-minded people. Also, there is the deterioration of the youthful native population who, very naturally, are inclined to copy the strange behaviour of these temporary immigrants. The Islanders used to be remarkable for their courtesy and good manners – alas, this trait is fast disappearing, owing to corruption from outside. Rudeness is mistaken for wit, and screaming and shouting for genuine enjoyment. Prevention is better than cure, and it would be wiser to stem this invasion quickly before the better class of residents are driven out of the Island."

Clara probably had to reach for the smelling salts as, one-by-one, a series of camps were opened all across the Island. By the late 1940s there were camps at Gurnard Pines, Bramble Chine, Brighstone and Yarmouth. They were joined by others in the fifties and sixties, including two camps side by side at Puckpool and St Clare - but the largest of the camps by far were the two that opened at Wootton. Little Canada, which had begun in the 1930s, was bought by Pontins in the late 1950s and they enlarged the camp to take advantage of the boom in holiday camps. Just along the road from them was Warner's Woodside Holiday Camp, equally large and successful, so much so that in 1969 Hovertravel even provided a Saturday hovercraft service direct to the camps, landing on a concrete apron on the beach at Woodside Bay.

Fancy dress night for staff at the Brambles Holiday Camp, Freshwater, probably in the 1940s or early 50s.

Across Britain, holiday camps became a part of the British way of life and it seemed they would go on forever, but it was not to be. Always hovering in the background, cheap package holidays abroad now became a serious threat to the camps. The tipping point came in the mid-seventies when a holiday abroad cost nearly the same as a holiday at home. The choice was simple. Was it Skegness, Bernie Clifton and egg and chips or Benidorm, Bacardi and sunshine. It was, as they say, a no-brainer - and it was the beginning of the end for the camps.

Warners made the first move and sold Woodside to Grand Metropolitan in 1981 but by then it was too late, holiday camps had well and truly lost their fizz, and when a serious fire destroyed the main complex four years later, Grand Met called it a day and closed the camp. The site then stood derelict for thirty years until it was sold in 2010 to become the Woodside Bay Lodge Retreat, a collection of high-end lodges set in unspoilt woodland, a sympathetic and imaginative development that still arouses passions to this day.

Pontin's Little Canada managed to struggle on for a few more years but finally closed in 1994, taking with it the cafe that had stood on the beach at Woodside for nearly fifty years. The camp site is now a children's activity centre operated by PGL.

Camps still exist at Bembridge, Yarmouth, Whitecliff Bay, Thorness, Nodes Point, and St Helens, but the lodges of yesterday have been replaced by static caravans. Today, seventy years after Clara tried to "stem this invasion," the sites, now re-branded as 'holiday parks' are as busy as ever.

Part of an early 60s brochure for the Little Canada camp.

by Brian Greening

Just after the Second World War, Arnolds Fair would be set up once a year at Seaclose recreation ground, and as I lay in bed just one hundred yards away, I knew just when it was shutting, as each evening the last tune played was Land of Hope and Glory. By 1952, a time when I was too young to chase girls but too old to go shopping with my mother, the event that my school pals and I looked forward to each year was Newport's annual carnival and the arrival of the fair at the triangle of grass next to Newport Football Club's pitch off Medina Avenue.

The fair was a great glitter magnet, all bright lights, and music pumping from a huge pneumatic organ. Add to

Mr. R. Pollington and Miss Norah Marshall grandstanding as our king and queen for Newport's 1933 carnival.

that the swing boats, the chair-o-planes, bumper cars, the inevitable roundabout with beautifully sculpted horses and the various sideshows. These included the 'hubbly bubbly' stall, manned by a young man with a thin moustache, a gammy leg and black hair smoothed down with a handful of Brylcreem that made him look like the comedian Arthur English, a detail wasted on the younger generation. "Roll up, roll up, Bob's your uncle, Fanny's your aunt," he would cry. The crowd would yell back with great gusto something a little risque and then everyone fell about laughing. His next shout was: "Hubbly, bubbly," which he would cry out continually until sufficient patrons crowded around, holding those little mesh nets into which the balls could be caught. A foot-pressed, air-blown machine then whirled multi-coloured table tennis balls into the air. The winner was the first to catch three balls. Plastic ducks could be shot with an air rifle, darts thrown to hit three playing cards or wooden hoops over jars of sweets, made all the more difficult because they were mounted on square wooden blocks.

The scene was complete. An old school colleague described it as follows. "There were great steam engines panting away, like elephants with St Vitus dance, that powered everything and the whole site was a veritable little city of flashing coloured lights, a Las Vegas in miniature on the edge of Newport," words that described the scene perfectly. I nearly forgot that there was also a cheerful little coloured man who would try to accurately guess your weight to within a few pounds, which he invariably did. If he failed, there was a cheap ring as a prize that could be passed on to a sister or some young lady who took your eye. It was a scene of complete merriment.

Nearly fifteen years ago I purchased around two hundred postcards of Newport's pre-war carnivals and eventually incorporated them into a book. They told of days long before political correctness and in 1924 one carnival entry even depicted two members of the Ku Klux Klan. The fair always attended the annual carnival. Almost every other parent spent time making costumes for their children. Too old to mind the ridicule I will get now, I entered one year and won third prize as a Shredded Wheat boy.

My good friend Fred Bolton as the 'Old Woman Who Lived in a Shoe'.

Who was this Mary with her lamb?

Different times have different values. Here, Newport firemen enter the carnival as 'The Dark Town Fire Brigade.

The Crinoline Lady towered above the crowds on her tour of Newport.

The children would gather in Quay Street and no offence was taken, or ever imagined, as boys dressed up as Zulu warriors, gollies and witch doctors. Girls costumes ranged from little Dutch girls, nursery rhyme characters like Little Miss Muffet or Hawaiian dancers with grass skirts or Gypsy ladies. Many of these entries would be frowned on today but nobody ever took offence. Once assembled, a parade of the streets took place, always ending at Church Litten. Judging inevitably resulted in the daughter of the Carnival Committee chairman winning a first prize but no competitor left empty handed, as even the losers were given a tin of toffees. A good friend of mine, Fred Bolton, would, in years to come, complain that his mother always entered him as a member of the opposite sex and I have a photo of him, see opposite, as the 'Old Woman Who Lived in a Shoe.'

Newport Victoria Sports Club entry showing just one side of a box of Christmas crackers.

Then it was hurry home, a quick snack and back to line the streets for the evening procession. Mrs. Brodie, a local gypsy lady, would sell carnival hats, sawdust-filled balls on a piece of elastic and paper wavers. Local traders, like Mew Langtons brewery, entered a float that often simply advertised their business, and farmers brought a horse-drawn wagon into town with a couple of sheep and a few bales of hay on board, enough to convince the spectators it was harvest time. The Women's Institute provided an entry that invariably had a classical theme and the local fire brigade entered with blackened faces as the 'Dark Town Fire Brigade', yet another entry that would be unacceptable today. There were bands aplenty, invariably including one from the Army barracks at Parkhurst and several town bands. Collectors in fancy dress rattled their tins and used long canvas funnels to collect donations from those watching in upstairs windows. The entire parade was led by the Carnival King and Queen, sitting majestically on high on a tractor-driven float, something that today would be banned on grounds of health and safety. Then it was back to the football ground, where a series of events took place in front of the main grandstand. There were marching displays, pram races with the baby invariably being a thirty-year-old dressed in a bonnet and romper suit with a dummy in his mouth, propelled by his drunken friend. There was community singing too. After the Second World War the community singing was led by Arthur Caiger DCM. Dressed in a white suit, it was he who conducted singing each year, from 1947 until 1962, at the FA Cup Final at Wembley. No doubt at great expense, Arthur was hired to perform at some of Newport Carnival's postwar events. The finale was a grand firework display. Then it was time to trudge wearily home once again, with the treat of buying a bag of chips from the shop on Coppins Bridge. A simple pleasure ending a wonderful day.

A nun with her friend Napoleon.

by Alan Stroud

Christmas comes but once a year. It's probably just as well, what with the sprouts and awkward walks around people holding collection boxes. And then there's the Christmas cracker jokes which, as we all know, are no laughing matter. The corny one-liners have a long pedigree but today they've moved with the times : "How will Christmas dinner be different after Brexit? – No Brussels" and "What do you call a man who's been diagnosed with attention deficit disorder? – These are good crackers, aren't they; who bought these?"

At the Front in 1916, if the bullets didn't kill you there were always the cigarettes.

Back in Victorian times, at Christmas the *County Press* hoisted up its skirt and let itself go - well, a bit. The 1892 Christmas edition offered up these groaners, under the title, 'Christmas Crackers' : What pudding makes the best cricketer? - A good batter. What is bought by the yard and worn by the foot? – A carpet. Well, titter ye not perhaps, but any of those would pass muster in today's crackers. In fact this one, from Christmas 1914, is still doing the rounds 100 years later, "MacBull : The wife's gone for a holiday to the West Indies. – O'Bear : Jamaica? - MacBull : No, it was her own idea."

Something else that hasn't changed are po-faced local politicians who have a monopoly on being right. It had been a long standing tradition that on Christmas Day the inmates of the Workhouse at Parkhurst were given some beer. Not in 1895 though. The practice was forbidden by the Board of Guardians, a committee of the local great and good who oversaw the running of the Workhouse. The *County Press* spoke out : "As far as we are aware the concession has never been abused, while there is abundant evidence that it has been very much enjoyed by many of the poorer old souls in the House. The Guardians refused to allow the Master to provide beer this Christmas.

It's 1956 and there's just the BBC to watch until ITV arrived in the South in 1958.

But surely, they would not refuse to allow it to be supplied by a generous friend outside? But this is just what they have done. The Mayor of Newport offered to provide ale on Christmas Day. The rejection of the offer was moved by a Guardian who said, "The inmates were very much better without it, both physically and mentally." How does he know that? Abstinence may be good for him but it does not necessarily follow that it is equally good for the rest of the human race. However, it is useless arguing with their stinginess. We leave them to reflect that they have curtailed the innocent pleasure of the poorest and most helpless class of the community."

Things were a lot friendlier twenty years later, in of all places, the trenches of the Somme. In a letter dated December 26th, 1914, Private Alan Conacher, serving at the Front, wrote a letter to his parents in Ryde who passed it on to the *County Press* : "Just after Christmas lunch we were very much surprised to see the Germans leave their trenches and come halfway to meet us. They gave us cigars and we gave them cigarettes, &c. They shook hands with us, wished us a merry Christmas and asked us not to fire for three days. We told them we would not if they did not. I had a chat with some, who spoke English very well. They said they were fed up with the war. Some of them were very fine men. Their officers exchanged greetings

"Parade" would have been the magazine of choice for many boys in the 60s. In second place the object of their lust would probably have been the Tri-ang catalogue

Christmas, 1924 style.

with our officers. Not a shot was fired the whole day.... I sat outside my dug-out that night and cooked two kippers in the flame of a candle, very much contented with my Christmas day. But fancy, in the greatest war in creation, going out to have a chat with the enemy and the next day we might be killing each other..."

Twenty years later, in 1935, it was generally accepted that another war was on the way but the Christmas jokes still kept on coming: Betty : "Mummy, what happens to a motor-car when it is too old to run?" Mother : "Someone sells it to your father."

A few years later, war came for a second time. There was no Instagram or Youtube in those far off days and no television so children, perish the thought, had to actually make their own entertainment. On the Island in 1942 some of them played that well known game and perennial favourite 'Find A Bomb And Throw Stones At It Until it Explodes' – As you do. The *County Press* reported, "Seeing a mortar bomb on the downs on Christmas Day, Edward and Raymond Ridett of Totland, aged 13 and 11, pelted it with stones until there was an explosion, and they were both wounded in the face and legs, fortunately not seriously. On Monday, Gordon Spirit, aged 14, of Madeira Road, found another bomb. He tried to unscrew the top and then threw it against a large stone, whereupon it exploded, wounding him in the leg, and he is now in the County Hospital."

In January 1945, when the war was all but over, this sad report pointed out how children had been denied a childhood during the war years, "On Wednesday evening the parents of five families, who wished to give their young people a New Year's treat, decided to pool their resources and give a joint party in the Unity-hall, Newport. With an inspiration which almost amounted to genius, the organiser decided to engage a Punch and Judy exhibition. The result was electrifying. Owing to five years of war, none of the toddlers had ever seen the renowned pair. They sat open-mouthed, drinking in every word of the dialogue, and shrieking with laughter as Punch belaboured all and sundry. It was a scene to delight the heart of Charles Dickens, but it was also a reminder of what the war has cost our children in hours of lost happiness."

by Alan Stroud

In a past life I was a telephone engineer. To coin a phrase, I've met the public, I've been round their house.

Back in the seventies, on one of those cold frosty morning mornings when you could see your breath on the air, I had to to fix the phone of the Rev. Eyton-Jones, in the vicarage at Queen's Road, Cowes. I parked outside and knocked on the door. It was opened by his housekeeper who led me down a flight of stairs to the basement kitchen where the elderly and jovial Rev. was sat at the table, in braces and dog collar, vigorously tucking into his breakfast - a pair of kippers. The Rev. was a nice old chap but a bit of a chatterbox and in between scoffing his kippers he talked pretty well non-stop while I repaired the phone.

When I finished and went to leave, he got up and followed me, still in full flow. He led the way up the stairs, past engravings hanging on the walls and stopped at each one to deliver a short lecture on it. It took ten long minutes to reach the top of the stairs, where I eventually opened the street door, thinking I was free at last.

However, the Rev. wasn't done yet and he followed me to the back of the van, still nattering, while I put my tools away. I turned to face him, thinking I was never going to get away, when suddenly it happened - he coughed. And as he coughed, a lump of something flew from his mouth, sailed through the air in an elegant curve and made a perfect crash-landing on my shoulder.

Straining to see out of the corner of my eye, I could just see the UFO. It was a lump of warm, chewed kipper, which to my surprise actually steamed in the cold frosty air for a brief moment. The Rev. could see it too. "Right ... well ... mustn't hold you up any longer," and he scurried indoors leaving me to flick his piscatorial friend off my shoulder. I have never looked a kipper in the eye since.

I got called out to the race results centre in Bath Road one evening during Cowes Week in 1984. In the foyer, along with a gaggle of Hooray Henrys, was an elderly, very upper-class lady on reception duty who spoke in a very high-pitched 'jolly hockey sticks' voice. I asked her where the faulty phone was but she knew nothing about it. She then headed off up the stairs, with me in tow, flying from room to room to try and find it; I checked each phone as we went. Eventually we came to a room with a man in. He was squatting on the floor studying sheets of paper spread out in front of him; he had a telephone pressed to his ear and in an Australian accent spoke excitedly ... "It was perfect weather on the Solent as the yachts lined up. I could see our boys there waiting for the off..." Quite oblivious to the signs that something was going on, Mrs Squeaky-voice barked loudly, "Is this telephone working correctly?" He completely ignored her and carried on reading what was obviously a script. She tried again, "Is this phone working properly? Only I've got the telephone man here who is looking for a faulty instrument." Again, he didn't stop talking but his time he showed great displeasure by waving his hand violently at her, motioning for her to be quiet and go away.

Anyone else would have got the message but I fear Mrs Squeaky-voice was made of sterner stuff. She squawked at him a third time in a voice that could shatter glass, "Can you tell me please, is this instrument working?"

He knew when he was beaten. He stopped talking, glared

From left to right, Ian Stephens, Len Hickman and Barry Guy on the steps of Newport Exchange in Crocker Street, December 1986. Above them (and inset) is a rarity, the royal crest of Edward VIII, 'The King that never was,' The exchange was one of just six public buildings commissioned during his 11 month reign before his abdication.

darkly at her and said, very slowly and precisely in a controlled voice, "I am in the middle of a live broadcast on Australian national radio. There is nothing wrong with this phone!" Quite unfazed at this revelation, she boomed in a foghorn voice, "Oh, right you are then, must be another one. Okay. Well, we'll leave you to it, then," and swept out of the room. The man rolled his eyes at me and spoke into the phone, "Now, where were we?" ... A wonderful moment which it would be nice to think still exists on an Australian radio outtakes tape.

I called at a house one day, knocked the door and waited but there was no reply. After knocking a few times I knelt down, lifted the letterbox flap and looked in. I found I was looking into a long hall, and at that precise moment an attractive woman in her mid-thirties coming out of what must have been her bedroom. I had obviously woken her up and she was in the act of pulling her nightdress together and she was in the process of ladling her naked breasts into the nightdress. To my horror she could obviously see a pair of eyes looking at her through her letterbox. I pulled my fingers out so quickly that I caught them on the letterbox flap and took the skin off my knuckles. The letterbox closed with a loud 'flap' and as I stood up, she opened the door. She knew that I'd seen, and I knew that she knew I'd seen. I said, "Good morning, telephone engineer," and being British, we carried on as if nothing had happened.

Finally, a story which my granddaughter, Leah, never tires of hearing. I went to a very posh house in the yachty area of Cowes one day - all thick carpets and antiques. The owner was a man with an equally posh, cultured voice, and he was not alone. With him in the room was a huge Great Dane, as big as a pony. He was a soppy, friendly thing and lolloped over to see me as I knelt down to work on the phone and then decided to use me as a scratching post. He leaned against me, his shoulder against mine, and very slowly drew the entire length of his body past me and then, as his rear end passed within inches of my face, he broke wind quite violently.

Now, I knew you worked your way inwards with the cutlery when you had a posh five-course meal but I wasn't quite sure what the etiquette was when a dog blew off at you. I was still pondering the point, reflecting that it brought a new meaning to the phrase 'feeling the wind in your face' when the man broke the pregnant silence by purring in his lovely dark-brown voice, "Bruce - You dirty bugger!"

Ryde exchange goes automatic in 1936

Maintenance engineer Bob Green checks all is in order in Cowes Exchange in1981.

A new electronic exchange is brought into service at Cowes in May, 1983. From l to r, Barry Hammond, Andy Hayward and Cyril Bridle. On phone at back, Peter Dibbens.

by Brian Greening

Thirty or more years ago I used to talk to a couple of local men who in their youth had been great sportsmen, achieving things I could only dream about. They were Jack Barton and Austin Stone, who via athletics became great rivals and, I am pleased to say, great friends. I compiled a book on Jack Barton's colourful life at his request, 'Jack Barton, Mr. Shalfleet,' and in it he told not only of his life but also of some of his sporting youth.

In one chapter Jack spoke of his great rival Austin, and admitted if a cross country course was over muddy, ploughed fields, there was nobody in the south of England to compare with his rival. Jack also told of how after winning the Hampshire one mile championship in 1933 he was selected to represent the county at the White City

Those great rivals Austin Stone and Jack Barton in a photo taken around 1933.

Another fine local athlete and rival of our two stalwarts was Cyril Price seen running through the ford at Carisbrooke.

in London. On the day, he left home at six o'clock and cycled from Shalfleet to Newport where a car took him to Ryde Pier and the boat trip to Portsmouth, then a train to Waterloo and then the underground to White City. After that preparation he not surprisingly failed to win, it was hardly the preparation one would follow today.

To be such fine athletes, it appears to go with the territory that both men were great characters. Sadly, Austin's latter days were seen out in a residential home on Newport Mall. One day he was asked if he was happy living there and replied that he was not. He was then asked if he had ever considered living at Bembridge to which he replied, "Bembridge! Bembridge! If I was a bird I wouldn't fly there." He later volunteered information that there had only ever been two people in his life that he hated, and that they were both Margaret Thatcher. Jack and Austin were two men that I am delighted to have met.

For many years Keith Mitchell, a lifelong friend and sporting colleague of mine, has periodically told me the story of a by the name of W.H. Croucher who scored the first century in a cricket match at Victoria Recreation ground, Newport, in 1902. He recently elaborated upon the story by telling me that it was current centurion Neil Shutler, Newport Cricket Club's Life Vice President, and Keith himself, who some years ago discovered an old cricket bag to which was attached a brass plaque that appeared to commemorate Mr. Croucher's feat but left a few questions unanswered. Sadly, the bag was beyond repair but the plaque was retained. It stated that it had been presented by P.H.A. to the recipient but he was unaware who the donors were. After twenty minutes of research in the *County Press* archives the full story emerged, and an interesting one it is. In July 1902, a cricket match took place between a Newport Cricket Club eleven and a team representing past and present pupils of Portland House Academy, a small private school situated at the top of West Street in Newport, where many important businessmen of the town gained their education. It appears that it was Mr. Croucher's ex-school that commemorated his achievement by presenting him with that cricket bag. On the day, the century maker was in top form and was eventually caught on the boundary after scoring 125 runs, supported by J.H. Williams who made 84 out of their team's total of 283 runs,

The brass plate from the cricket bag presented to Mr. Croucher to celebrate his achievement.

this being at the time another record, the highest number of runs scored in an innings at that venue. In reply, the Newport team were dismissed for just 53 runs, with H.F. Scott and C.J. Minns taking five wickets apiece. To many, a story of little interest but it was indeed yet another piece of local history that needed recording.